# TABLE OF CONTENTS

# INTRODUCTION

The subject of Joint Close Air Support (JCAS) has a long history of interservice tension and competing interests. Both scholars and military members alike have deliberated and studied the role of JCAS in warfare, examining which service should execute the role and which aircraft is best suited to perform the mission. The armed forces will have to address a far more significant issue in the near future concerning the planning and employment of JCAS, beyond the simplistic considerations of apportionment, allocation, and effects. Because of the increased lethality and proliferation of surface-to-air threats, the operational environment is changing. This reality requires a greater amount of detail and specificity during operational planning. In addition, the United States will inevitably have to rely on a smaller, multi-role air component with fewer aircraft. In an interview on 26 January 2012, Vice Chairman of the Joint Chiefs of Staff, Admiral James A. Winnefeld, Jr. stated, ""Is the F-35 going to be as good a close-air support platform as an A-10? I don't think anybody believes that, but is the A-10 going to be the air-to-air platform that the F-35 is going to be? So again, the Air Force is trying to get as much multimission capability into the limited number of platforms it's going to have."[1]

In order to ensure dominating tactical execution, the land and air components must shift away from the current JCAS practices based on no air threat and negligible

---

[1] Jeff Schogol, "5 A-10 squadrons to be cut, Tight budgets lead AF to focus on F-35 capabilities," *Air Force Times*, 30 January 2012, http://www.airforcetimes.com/article/20120130/NEWS/201300303/5-A-10-squadrons-to-be-cut (accessed 17 January 2013).

competing interests between close air support and strategic strike that have been become commonplace during Operation ENDURING FREEDOM and Operation IRAQI FREEDOM.

Essential connections between the Joint Force Land Forces Component Commander (JFLCC) and that of the Joint Force Air Component Commander (JFACC) must be defined clearly, established early, and sustained throughout the planning and execution phases of any operational plan. The shared relationship between the JFLCC and JFACC, while historically important, will be even more critical in an environment of competing doctrine. The success of JCAS in the future operational environment will hinge upon the operational planners' ability to construct an operational framework that facilitates effective JCAS employment led by an integrated JFLCC/JFACC team in a unified effort.

## The Emerging Operational Environment

Enemy threat systems to air assets in future campaigns will be more pervasive and lethal. This global threat is proliferating and is becoming increasingly difficult to mitigate, presenting greater risk for tactical aircraft. Surface-to-air-missiles (SAM) are increasing in both sophistication and quantity. The growing number of SAMs, combined with anti-aircraft-artillery (AAA), and near-peer fighter aircraft are creating a significant anti-access/area denial (A2/AD) environment, especially for fighter-bomber aircraft supporting ground forces.[2] The combined effect of threat capability directed against a smaller air component with multiple mission requirements creates the need for new thinking on the execution of JCAS in any future campaign. The increased enemy-threat system architecture will require additional planning to employ CAS. Planning will include providing the necessary command and control (C2) assets and joint suppression of enemy air defense assets (JSEAD) apportioned to a JCAS mission to reduce fighter-bomber exposure times.[3] Given this threat environment to aircraft, it would be foolish to not consider a paradigm shift for close air support; fighter-bomber aircraft will not be able to hold over the target area in a "CAS stack," while building situational awareness, nor will aircraft be able to refuel with a tanker directly over the battlefield.[4] Likewise, the land component, so long accustomed to having continuous JCAS coverage with the added benefit of readily available on-call alert aircraft, will have to adapt to delayed support while the air component strikes essential long range operational and strategic target sets.

As potential future air threats grow in lethality and availability, the air component will also become smaller and more diversified.[5] The 2012 Defense Strategic Guidance

---

[2] Nathan Freier, "The Emerging Anti-Access/Area Denial Challenge,"*Center of Strategic and International Studies*, 17 May 2012, http://csis.org/publication/emerging-anti-accessarea-denial-challenge (accessed 18 January 2013).

[3] U.S. Joint Chiefs of Staff, *Joint Airspace Control*, Joint Publication 3-52 (Washington, D.C.: Joint Chiefs of Staff, 20 May 2010), III-9.

[4] From the author's experience during Operation IRAQI FREEDOM as operations transitioned from Phase III to Phase IV, the "CAS stack" became a non-doctrinal moniker for multiple aircraft holding above a close air support engagement area, waiting for an opportunity to employ. The "CAS stack" was oriented directly over the battlefield since there was little to no threat of anti-aircraft systems.

[5] The Department of Defense budget will be decreasing significantly over the next ten years. The overall effect of these budget cuts will result in a smaller force size across the services. Included in these force cuts are proposals to retire five squadrons of A-10Cs (equating to 102 aircraft) and a squadron of F-

states that the Department of Defense must relook at its core competencies as the United States prepares to deal with fiscal constraints.[6] Budget cuts now and in the future will affect both friendly air-asset force size and friendly air-asset composition. The United States has been fortunate to enjoy the benefits of dominate designed weapons systems in a specific domain or mission set, but as the Defense Guidance implies and the Air Force has stated, future air assets will be, by necessity, more multi-role in nature. The reduction in attack role aircraft, like the A-10C, and the reductions in total fighter-bomber aircraft will result in both a smaller air component that must not only provide support to ground forces, but must also execute several other missions.[7] These missions include long-range strategic strike where the air component attacks decisive targets deep in enemy held territory, interdiction missions where the air component engages logistics and supply lines supporting the enemies fielded forces, and air superiority missions where the air component neutralizes enemy air-to-air threats and surface-to-air threats.[8]

Historical evidence shows that close air support specialty aircraft provided the preponderance of close support to ground forces and multi-role fighter-bomber aircraft

---

16's (an additional 21 aircraft). The A-10C retirements comprise 29 percent of the total A-10C fleet, whose primary mission is providing Joint Close Air Support and supporting ground forces via Forward Air Controlling and multiple other missions. Projections also forecast a one hundred to eight hundred fighter/bomber aircraft shortfall by 2024 based upon the retirement of aging legacy fighters and stagnate new fighter production. See John Tirpak, "Rising risk in the fighter force," *Air Force Magazine*, February 2010 http://www.airforcemag.com/MagazineArchive/Pages/2010/February%202010/0210fighter.aspx (accessed 18 January 2013).

[6] Department of Defense, *Sustaining U.S. Global Leadership: Priorities for 21st Century Defense* (Washington, D.C.: U.S. Department of Defense, January 2012), 3.

[7] Rowan Scarborough, "Fleets fade away with Pentagon budget cuts," *The Washington Times*, 5 February 2012, http://www.washingtontimes.com/news/2012/feb/5/fleets-fade-away-with-pentagon-budget-cuts/#.UPiys8lORoQ.email (accessed 18 January 2013).

[8] U.S. Air Force, *Counterland Operations*, Air Force Doctrine Document 3-03 (Washington, D.C.: U.S. Air Force, 11 September 2006 (Change 1, 28 July 2011), 4.

were free to accomplish interdiction and strategic strike missions. However, a smaller, more multi-role force has significant implications for the future Joint Force Commander (JFC). Operational planners and command and control entities currently assign fighter-bomber aircraft to JCAS missions via an apportionment system, leaving multi-role aircraft to conduct other missions.[9] The shift to a smaller air component expected to do all missions with one type of multi-role aircraft requires a major change in planning for joint campaigns. The current apportionment system will be forced to balance competing mission sets constantly. It is essential now to define the critical planning and leadership considerations associated with JCAS operations with limited air assets in a high threat environment.

## JCAS Operational Planning: Outlining the Approach

There are a series of assumptions that are required in order to frame the argument. The first assumption is that the air component will be comprised of generic fighter-bomber aircraft as the force size is reduced. The second assumption is that the campaign will be executed within a high threat or A2/AD area of operations. The third assumption is that the land component will require significant close air support from the air component. While utilizing air power to support ground forces has evolved from conflict to conflict, there have been consistent themes that have presented themselves. These themes capture both the core concepts for leadership and operational planning that are necessary for future campaigns as well as recurring themes where the air and land

---

[9] Ibid., 44.

components were not integrated. Therefore, a historical review of close air support operations and the role of leadership in those operations are essential to draw the required operational planning tenets and keys for successful leadership when planning and executing close air support. Operational leaders should then adhere to these tenets and ensure the joint planning team incorporates them into the joint planning process to achieve a comprehensive approach in balancing and integrating strategic strike with close air support and ground maneuver.

## CHAPTER 2:  AN HISTORICAL ANALYSIS OF JCAS

In order to derive key factors to assist in determining the future of JCAS in the joint campaign, this historical analysis will address the operational planning aspects essential to effective JCAS and the associated operational leader characteristics necessary to implement JCAS as part of an operational design.  The analysis provides examples assessing successes and failures in operational planning to integrate ground operations with corresponding air support.  The analyses will also highlight the importance of relationships between leaders in both planning and conducting a campaign.

### World War I

As war broke out across Europe in 1914, France, Great Britain, Germany, and Italy had made considerable advancements transitioning the role of aircraft from observation and reconnaissance to weapons delivery and attack.[1]  While the air component was trying to determine its role in warfare, the 1914 U.S. Army Field Service Regulations stated, "the infantry is the principal and most important arm" and thereby relegated the other combat functions of artillery, cavalry, and the newly emerging role of airpower to a subordinate support role."[2]  From this single regulation stems much of today's friction concerning the relationship of supported and supporting, with the

---

[1] U.S. Army, "A Short History of Close Air Support Issues" (Fort Berlvoir, VA: Headquarters U.S. Army Combat Developments Command Institute of Special Studies, July 1968), 2.

[2] John Schlight, *Help from Above:  Air Force Close Air Support of the Army 1946 - 1973* (Washington, D.C.: Air Force History and Museums Program, 2003), 3.

associated role of defining a main effort that have plagued operational planners and leaders.

With the entry of the United States into the war in 1917, the first controversies between the air component and ground component began to materialize. Colonel William "Billy" Mitchell, Chief of Air Services, did not hide his dissatisfaction with "non-flyers" making critical decisions involving air missions.[3] Mitchell often directed his frustration towards ground corps commanders who, in his view, were unfamiliar with the capabilities and limitations of close air support.[4] Mitchell also expressed frustration that infantry commanders did not understand the capabilities of aircraft used to attack against enemy strategic targets or the importance of interdicting supply lines and logistical staging areas.[5]

Conversely, ground commanders had their own share of frustrations concerning the Air Service. These frustrations often stemmed from the ground commander's perception of an aerial culture of individualism and lack of discipline that manifested itself with a lack of air support, corps commanders complained that the only aircraft they ever saw were German.[6] The air component appeared to fly by, or ignore, ground targets that had been persistently holding up friendly forces.[7] This lack of understanding led to a

---

[3] Schlight, *Help from Above*, 5.

[4] Ibid.

[5] Ibid. In one specific disagreement Colonel Mithchell's dissatisfaction with ground commander taskings became so heated that General John J. Pershing had to intervene and save the relationship from completely deteriorating.

[6] Ibid., 11.

[7] Ibid., 12.

lack of trust between operational leaders and created an initial fissure between the air

component and land components belief in how best to wage warfare.[8]

## Interwar Period World War I to World War II

Many of the initial strains evident between the air component and the ground

component remained and were even compounded in the interwar period.  One of the

outcomes was the evolution of the air service into two distinct functions, that of tactical

missions and strategic missions (due in large part to Mitchell's development of doctrine

and direction at the time).[9]  With the divergence into these two categorical functions

came additional debates over whether strategic and tactical missions required separate

functioning aircraft or if one type of mission could fulfill both roles.[10]

Evolutions in technology and the development of a new air strategy created

additional friction.  In 1921, Giulio Douhet released his canonic, *The Command of the

Air*, in which he focused entirely on strategic bombing and its cumulative effects on a

campaign.[11]  Douhet not only eschewed supporting using air power to support ground

forces, but even went so far as to posit that such support could be detrimental to the

overall war effort.[12]  Billy Mitchell published *The Provisional Manual for the*

---

[8] U.S. Army, "A Short History," 3.

[9] U.S. Air Force, "An Executive Brief on the Development of Close Air Support Doctrine*"*
(Headquarters Tactical Air Command: Doctrine Division Directorate of Concepts, Doctrine, Policy and
Studies, 5 January 1972), 3.

[10] U.S. Army, "A Short History," 5.

[11] Julio Douhet, *The Command of the Air* (North Stratford, NH: Ayer Company Publishers, 2002),
20 - 9.

[12] Ibid., 251 – 9.

*Employment of Air Service* in 23 December 1918.[13]  In it, Mitchell purposed that at key

points within a battle, air support to ground operations was valid, but also asserted that

the majority of missions for air power, should be on strategic mission sets.  The Army

General Staff refuted this line of logic, stating the mission of air units "is to aid the

ground forces to gain decisive success" in essence, revalidating the 1914 concept of air

power.[14]  The Army Air Corps divided itself over Mitchell's approach.  Some believed

air power should be used to support maneuver warfare; others believed that strategic

attack was the most effective use of air power.[15]  The creation of pursuit and attack

squadrons reflected the Army general staff's resolve towards ground support.[16]  The

Army's predominant view at the time was that effects needed to be immediate and there

was little time nor concern to determine if interdicting an enemy's supply lines from the

air would have a positive or negative effect.[17]  Mitchell himself wrote the following

mission statement for the newly minted attack squadrons:

> During offensives, attack squadrons operate over and in front of the
> infantry and neutralize the fire of the enemy's infantry and barrage
> batteries.  On the defensive, the appearance of attack airplanes affords
> visible proof to heavily engaged troops that Headquarters is maintaining
> close touch with the front, and is employing all possible auxiliaries to
> support the fighting troops.[18]

---

[13] U.S. Air Force Historical Advisory Committee, *Case Studies in the Development of Close Air Support* (Washington, D.C.: Office of Air Force History United States Air Force, 1990), 42 – 3.

[14] War Department, "Fundamental Principles for the Employment of the Air Service," *Training Regulation No. 440-15* (Washington DC:  Air Service, 26 January 1926, 1.  Re-typed and re-formatted by the Air War College, http://www.au.af.mil/au/awc/awcgate/documents/tr440-15 htm (accessed 20 January 2013).

[15] U.S. Air Force, "Close Air Support Doctrine," 2.

[16] U.S. Air Force Historical Advisory Committee, *Close Air Support*, 43.

[17] U.S. Air Force, "Close Air Support Doctrine," 8.

[18] U.S. Air Force Historical Advisory Committee, *Close Air Support*, 43.

As the Army Air Corps continued to evolve and grow, Mitchell returned to his air centric previous position of limited air support to ground forces in favor of the air component being the sole decisive force in a campaign. Even after his retirement in 1930, Mitchell remained the consummate air power advocate; Mitchell saw little use for ground support missions in future war:

> This branch of aviation will have most of its application in the future against what are termed partisan or irregular troops, and as are found in Asia, Africa, Mexico, and Central America, that is those not equipped with large air forces and which do not move in large numbers but comparatively in small mobile detachments.[19]

Reflecting Mitchell's glum assessment, the Air Corps Tactical School's attack aviation curriculum 1939 stated that one should not attack within artillery range or against deployed troops, "except for cases of great emergency."[20] Joint training exercises were almost non-existent, primarily due to the lack of air assets.[21]

As the emphasis on air support waned, the focus on interdiction and strategic strike gained momentum. At the twilight of the 1930s, the Army Air Corps concentrated almost completely on strategic bombing campaigns.[22] Starting in 1935, the Air Corps Tactical School would rename its attack courses light bombardment and would assert that the most effective way of supporting ground forces was by assuring air supremacy.[23] Brigadier General Henry H. Arnold addressed the Army War College and passed on his

---

[19] Ibid., 46.

[20] Schlight, *Help from Above*, 22.

[21] John J. McGrath, *Fire for Effect: Field Artillery and Close Air Support in the US Army* (Fort Leavenworth, KS: Combat Studies Institute Press, 2010), 62 – 3.

[22] Schlight, *Help from Above*, 22.

[23] U.S. Air Force Historical Advisory Committee, *Close Air Support*, 52.

view on the use of air power in modern war. He praised Japan for not assigning air forces against front line forces in its recent engagements in China. Arnold concluded with the following dictum: "Do not detach the air force to small commands where it will be frittered away in petty fighting. Hold it centrally and use it in its proper place, that is, where it can exert its power beyond the influence of your other arms, to influence general action rather than specific battle."[24] Colonel Paul M. Rabinette, assigned to the General Staff in 1941 prior to the onset of the war summarized both Arnold's and the Army Air Force's thinking:

> His faith in heavy long range bombers was unbounded, and this faith carried into action gave the U.S. outstanding position in strategic aviation, and ultimately supremacy in the air. But there was little thought given to the ground troops or to their problems, second place going to pursuit type airplanes.[25]

Conversely, the Army was increasingly suspect if air power could truly be a critical factor in the outcome of engagement, much less be the deciding force in winning a war.[26] Germany's decisive combined arms Blitzkrieg with the support of the *Luftwaffe* (specifically *Stuka* ground support aircraft) sent the Army Air Corps scrambling for attack aviation assets and supporting doctrine for combined arms operations and close air support.[27] The Air Corps was shocked to discover how balanced the *Luftwaffe* was in its ability to provide both ground support and deep attack aircraft in a synchronized

---

[24] Ibid., 48.

[25] Ibid., 60.

[26] Ibid., 46.

[27] Schlight, *Help from Above*, 29 - 30.

campaign that caused the rapid defeat of every army it faced.[28] At the same time the Army Air Corps boasted a meager thirty bomber and pursuit squadrons, nineteen observation and reconnaissance squadrons, and a sparse seven attack squadrons.[29]

During the interwar period relationships between the air and ground forces deteriorated. Due in large part to a competition for resources and funding combined with opposing dogmatic beliefs; there was a significant lack of trust between the ground and the air components. This mistrust was reflected in the idea that only by assigning the command and control to a single ground commander could air power be effective.[30]

Unlike Mitchell and Arnold, ground commanders had little use for bombing targets away from the front lines. As a result there was very little operational planning, due to the air component's desire to execute only strategic strike missions.[31] At the onset of World War II, the air and land components would have to adapt and learn in the crucible of combat to derive the best practices for close air support.

## World War II

The British-United States landing in North Africa called Operation TORCH, illustrated the problems with close air support not solved in the interwar period. Operation TORCH depended on the Allied air forces gaining air superiority and attacking axis targets of operational and tactical value.[32] The Allied ground forces' linkage to the

---

[28] Ibid.

[29] Ibid., 22.

[30] U.S. Air Force Historical Advisory Committee, *Close Air Support*, 58.

[31] Ibid.

[32] U.S. Air Force, "Close Air Support Doctrine," 4.

Allied air command structure was a major point of contention, based on the differing concepts of envisioned use of air power.[33] The division between the land and air commanders created a fissure among the land and air component forces that fostered mistrust from the very outset and led to significant problems in execution. Air power planners and commanders were frustrated by the lack of strategic targets within the African theatre. There were few, if any, critical targets, enemy airfields were far out of reach, and supply lines and lines of communication were non-existent.[34]

Not surprisingly, the ground commanders desired the air component to provide localized air cover, and act as on-call long range artillery, attacking targets of opportunity, designated by the ground forces.[35] The air component believed it could provide better air cover by attacking enemy airfields and interdicting enemy reinforcements.[36] It was 1918 all over again: aircraft came under the direct control of the ground commander, who expected to have no enemy air threat and on-call close air support whenever needed. However, in practice, the air assets were either misapplied or not used at all due to procedural problems, poor planning and logistics, and conflicting command guidance. The inability of operational planners to synchronize air and ground operations doomed the campaign.

In February of 1943, the effectiveness of a combined air and land component continued to degrade. Major General Carl A. Spaatz, Commander Allied Northwest

---

[33] Ibid., 5.

[34] U.S. Air Force Historical Advisory Committee, *Close Air Support*, 164.

[35] Ibid., 169.

[36] Ibid.

14

Africa Air Forces, did not bolster the interconnectedness of the two services or devise a balanced strategy of support and interdiction while dealing with Major General Lloyd R. Fredendall, United States II Corps Commander.[37] The II Corps mission was to hold the eastern passes leading to Tunis to allow the Allies to mass artillery, armor, aircraft, and logistics.[38] Once the seasonal rains ended, the Allies would then break through the lines in in an effort to reach the eastern coast.[39] Fredendall had little understanding of the role of air power in battle, and Spaatz had little patience for Fredendall.[40] Fredendall told Spaatz he wanted forty-eight hours of air support prior to the commencement of operations.[41] Fredendall told Spaatz that he "wanted his men to see some bombs dropped on the positions immediately in front of them, and if possible, some dive bombers brought down in sight of his troops so their morale would be bolstered."[42] When Spaatz protested due to his pursuit and bomber squadrons being already tasked to their limits, Fredendall retorted that he had lost 300 men due to enemy actions and the lack of air support was unacceptable.[43] Spaatz argued that close air support was not the best use of air power, but it should instead be concentrated on air superiority and interdiction.[44] Most of the Twelfth Air Force attacks were allocated against enemy airfields, shipping

---

[37] Geoffery Perrett, *There is a War to be Won* (New York: Random House, 1991), 150 – 2.

[38] Ibid., 152.

[39] Ibid., 154.

[40] Ibid.

[41] U.S. Air Force Historical Advisory Committee, *Close Air Support*, 169.

[42] Ibid.

[43] Ibid.

[44] Ibid.

and supplies, very little of it went towards close air support.[45]  Predictably, Fredendall

thought the solution was for him to take direct control of the air component.[46]  The

fissure between the operational leaders continued to grow.  Both components envisioned

different priorities for their use and neither side was talking or listening to the other.  The

air component challenges were compounded by P-40s being matched against superior

German Me-109s, the inability to mass due to the capacity of their airfields, and

operating at the maximum limits of their range.[47]  The result of the lack of air and ground

integration stalled the II Corps attack and dramatically increased American casualties.[48]

The Americans would eventually reassess the command and control structure along with

mission objectives and priorities but not before enduring significant friction and tension

in the planning and executing joint operations.

In contrast to Spaatz and Fredendall, the relationship between Air Vice Marshall

Sir Arthur Coningham, commander of the Western Desert Air Force, and General

Bernard Montgomery, commander of the Eighth Army, provided a model of adaptability

and effectiveness.[49]  Montgomery understood that the intrinsic value of air power lay in

its flexibility to shift rapidly from one target to another.  He insisted that air and ground

planners should share the same headquarters, so that the air component could effectively

shift missions.[50]  Coningham took Montgomery's ideas, added his own views, and then

---

[45] Perrett, *War to be Won*, 154.

[46] U.S. Air Force Historical Advisory Committee, *Close Air Support*, 168.

[47] Ibid.

[48] Ibid., 169 - 70.

[49] Ibid., 172.

[50] Ibid.

distributed them for mandatory reading. Coningham later summarized these ideas into six tenets:

1) Air superiority is the first requirement for any major land operation

2) The strength of air power lies in its flexibility and capacity for rapid concentration

3) It follows that control must be concentrated

4) Air forces must be concentrated and not dispersed in penny packets

5) The commanders and their staffs must work together

6) The plan of operation should be mutually adjusted and combined from the start.[51]

Although, Coningham and Montgomery shared an understanding of the need for smart operational planning to facilitate successful air-ground execution, the Americans were far less adaptable. Major General George S. Patton, who replaced Fredendall after the Kasserine Pass debacle, became increasingly upset with the perceived lack of air support the II Corps received.[52] At this point in the campaign, the Germans maintained air superiority, as well as numerous forward airfields from which to operate.[53]

Patton, like Fredendall, had completely unrealistic expectations of air power. Patton was not appeased unless he could see allied aircraft attack enemy positions directly in front of him and little time or patience for the necessity of strategic strike missions. When his own staff was attacked during a German air raid, Patton began a scathing campaign up the chain of command relaying his perception of the air component

---

[51] Ibid., 174.

[52] Ibid., 175 - 7.

[53] Ibid., 177.

and its ineffectiveness.[54] The episode escalated to a point that General Dwight Eisenhower, the Commander of Allied Forces in North Africa, had to intercede to limit damage to the alliance.[55]

In an attempt to ease the problems over the role of air power, Army Chief of Staff General George C. Marshall directed the production of a new manual on the command and execution of air power which was released on 21 July 1943, Field Manual 100-20.[56] The field manual reflected two of Coningham's ideas regarding air power's flexibility and the ability of aircraft to mass against targets.[57] Its most pivotal concept attempted to overcome the air-land battle for supremacy. "Land and air power are coequal and interdependent forces; neither is an auxiliary of the other."[58] The new field manual would shape the conduct of future operations.

In addition to a new doctrine, General Marshall needed new officers to implement it. Major General Elwood R. (Pete) Quesada's quick rise in rank indicated that Marshall intended to bring new leaders the forefront, no matter how young or junior.[59] One could describe Quesada's personality as extroverted and charismatic (brushing on vain), with a drive for accomplishment that bordered on the self-serving.[60] What made Quesada different from other Air Corps generals, however, was his passion

---

[54] Ibid.

[55] Ibid., 178.

[56] U.S. Army, "Close Air Support Issues," 20 - 1.

[57] U.S. Air Force, "Close Air Support Doctrine," 6 - 7.

[58] U.S. Air Force Historical Advisory Committee, *Close Air Support*, 184 - 5.

[59] Thomas A. Hughes, *Overlord: General Pete Quesada and the Triumph of Tactical Air Power in World War II* (New York: The Free Press, 1995), 24.

[60] Ibid., 83 – 110.

for the tactical employment of aircraft in close air support. Quesada's experience in North Africa in 1942 and in Italy in 1943 shaped his belief in close air support.[61] While Quesada endorsed the importance of strategic attack, he felt it was essential for the air component to support ground forces.

During the two campaigns prior to Normandy, Quesada felt that the most direct impact air power could deliver was against enemy forces preparing to make contact with Allied ground forces. He saw that the relationships from the commander down to the individual pilot with the ground forces were one of the most critical elements of success. He also learned that the most effective way to plan was with by combining land and air planners into one planning team.[62]

Quesada assumed command of IX Fighter Command in October 1943, whose primary task would be close air support for the United States V and VII Corps with primarily tactical fighters including P-51 Mustangs, P-38 Lightnings, and P-47 Thunderbolts aircraft that, unlike the P-40, were more than a match for German fighters.[63] Quesada tackled the logistics and structure challenges of the new command and shifted to tactics and doctrine, with an emphasis on sound planning for employment.[64]

Quesada sought to establish a relationship with the ground commanders responsible for the assault during Operation NEPTUNE. Quesada made a concerted

---

[61] Ibid.

[62] Ibid.

[63] Ibid., 114.

[64] Ibid., 115.

effort with Major General Charles Gerhardt of the 29th Infantry Division.[65] Quesada hosted Gerhardt at a number of social gatherings, and shared his thoughts on close air support.[66] He worked diligently to meld his operational plan to the land components objectives. His focus on providing close air support in harmony with ground maneuver was clearly so different from his other Air Corps commanders that it seemed Quesada was creating his own Air Force.[67] Unlike Spaatz (now the Commander of Strategic Air Forces in Europe), General Hunter Harris Junior (Commander 13th Combat Wing of Eighth Air Force), and General James H. Doolittle (Eight Air Force Commander), who all were advocates of supporting the landings solely through strategic attacks, "Quesada's air force," as it was known, was wholly dedicated to the support of ground forces.[68] The land and air component finally agreed on the forces and functions for the invasion, but only after an intervention held by Eisenhower.[69] Quesada continued to plan and train as much as possible with the ground forces, building the pilot's skills in attacking ground targets in coordination with ground maneuver. He went as far as sending 227 of his pilots to the Mediterranean Theater so they could execute dive-bombing attacks, close air support tactics, as well as observe operational planning.[70]

The most effective relationship Quesada had with the land component commanders was with General Omar Bradley, the United States commander, 21st Army

---

[65] Ibid., 119.

[66] Ibid.

[67] Ibid., 121.

[68] Ibid., 121 – 3.

[69] Ibid., 128.

[70] Ibid.

Group.[71]  The common thread between the diverse generals was an extreme desire to win

the war and disregarding the air-ground tensions that continued to exist.  Their command

posts were co-located and their personal quarters were in the same vicinity.  Due to the

close relationship between Bradley and Quesada, the United States First Army and IX

Tactical Air Command created a system for planning and execution.  The two staffs

worked in coordination to determine the priority for the next day's events, ensured the

correct assets and forces were available, and planned for the time when close air support

was required.  The air-ground staff presented the plan to Bradley and Quesada, who

would then approve the plan.[72]

Due to inclement weather during the D-Day invasion, Quesada's air force was

unable to play a decisive role in the operation, but that did not dissuade Quesada from

attempting to make an impact.[73]  Shortly after the beach landing the Allies were able to

secure an area for an airfield in Normandy.  Quesada moved to the forward area, but kept

his tent close to Bradley's quarters.[74]  When inclement weather threatened cancelling

further air missions, Quesada would personally run out and direct flights were to go to

support the land component.[75]  He insisted his pilots rotate to the front lines so they could

understand the infantryman's perspective.[76]  As early as 18 June 1944, Quesada

impressed upon Bradley the need to concentrate his air component in mass and use

---

[71] Perrett, *War to be Won*, 334.

[72] Ibid.

[73] Hughes, *Overlord*, 141.

[74] Perrett, *War to be Won*, 334.

[75] Hughes, *Overlord*, 7 - 10.

[76] Perrett, *War to be Won*, 334.

"steamroller tactics" with massed armor to punch a hole through the German lines and counter the persistent issue of the French countryside hedgerows.[77] Prior to supporting major operations like the push into St.-Lo-Periers, Quesada would personally fly in the first wave to ensure the land component was receiving the support it needed.[78] The air land coordination became so good that the IX Tactical Air Command pilots were known for being able to safely bomb within 100 yards of friendly forces.[79]

General Dwight D. Eisenhower with Lieutenant General Omar Bradley and Major General Pete Quesada. (Photo from National Archives) http://www.armchairgeneral.com/ike-world-war-iis-indispensable-general-part-iii htm (accessed 1 February 2013)

---

[77] Ibid.

[78] Ibid., 337 – 8.

[79] Ibid., 334.

Quesada's Ninth soon became a model of success for others to emulate. During General George S. Patton's Third Army advance across France, the XIX Tactical Air Command, led by Brigadier General Otto P.Weyland, was created to support the ground maneuver.[80] Patton and Weyland soon shared a similar relationship to that of Bradley and Quesada. Weyland would use a combination of armed recce and close air support to facilitate Patton's maneuver against enemy forces.[81] By "isolating the battlefield" as they called it, air power would decimate everything the Germans tried to move to reinforce the front; what survived to make contact was dispatched in an efficient combined arms attack. The attacks became so devastating that at the town of Beugency, 20,000 German soldiers surrendered to an infantry platoon out of fear that they would come under an air attack if they stayed in the battlefield. [82]

The relationships between Bradley and Quesada and Patton and Weyland represent the desired model for air land leadership. The air component and land component had evolved beyond the division of the interwar period to develop a level of integration that proved to be decisive on the battlefield. The operational leadership was underpinned by a level of operational planning that paired the land component with the air component in such a manner as ensure success.

---

[80] Ibid., 366 - 7.

[81] Ibid., 367.

[82] Ibid.

## Korea

Between 1945 and 1950, the United States Air Force had finished its transition to become a separate service. With the Air Force's autonomy came a return to an emphasis on strategic targeting using nuclear weapons against the Soviet Union.[83] The commencement of hostilities in Korea caught the United States with a land and air component that was not prepared.[84] While there were vestiges of the advancements in close air support from World War II, the operational planning and command relationships suffered greatly.

At the onset of hostilities, the Army and Air Force concentrated on halting the massive North Korea invasion. For the first three weeks of the war, close air support dominated.[85] As United Nations forces advanced, the Air Force transitioned to interdiction and strategic bombing; the intervention of the Chinese required overwhelming close air support as the stalemate solidified along the 38th parallel, interdiction and strategic bombing dominated.[86] The front began to stabilize, and at the same time, the relationship between the land component and air component started to fracture. As it happened in 1918 and 1942, commanders could not agree on target priorities. Despite the establishment of an integrated team meant to select targets in support of Joint operations called the Joint Target Selection Board, the services could not

---

[83] Schlight, *Help from Above*, 118.

[84] U.S. Air Force Historical Advisory Committee, *Close Air Support*, 358.

[85] U.S. Army, "Close Air Support Issues," 37.

[86] Schlight, *Help from Above*, 120 - 2.

come to a consensus on the best use of air power.[87] At the very forefront of the friction was Lieutenant General Otto P. Weyland, Commander Far East Air Forces, against Major General Edward M. Almond, Commander X Corps, in a contest of wills.[88]

General Almond's overarching priority, following the FM 100-20 doctrine, was for the air component to gain air superiority.[89] Once achieved, he believed the Air Force's only responsibility should be to support the ground forces while under the command of the land component.[90] In contrast, Weyland believed the focus should be on interdiction of enemy lines of communication and supply and assembly areas followed by support to the ground forces once they were preparing to make contact with the enemy. Weyland's use of air power to attack lines of communication was formed during World War II supporting Patton's Third Army.[91] While General Almond understood the importance of interdicting supply lines and logistical areas, he did not believe that those missions should degrade the priority for close air support in any form or fashion.[92] Just as previous commanders had done in 1942, General Almond attempted to take control of the air component at every opportunity. Almond accused the Air Force of only

---

[87] Ibid., 124.

[88] Ibid., 136.

[89] U.S. Air Force Historical Advisory Committee, *Close Air Support*, 361.

[90] Ibid.

[91] Schlight, *Help from Above*, 136.

[92] Major Michael Lewis, "Lt Gen Ned Almond, USA, A Ground Commander's Conflicting View with Airmen over CAS Doctrine and Employment" (Maxwell Air Force Base, AL: Air University, School of Advanced Airpower Studies 1997), 53.

exercising their flexibility in taking away close air support assets instead of providing them.[93]

Unfortunately, the Air Forces operational plan to provide close air support focused primarily on a simplistic pre-planned request and apportionment system.[94] The rigidness of this system and the lack of integration between the operational leaders led the Army to perceive that close air support in Korea lacked unity of command and flexibility of planning and execution. Like General Patton in 1943, General Almond's conflict with his air component counterpart reached a crescendo in 1950 when he penned a scathing letter to the Chief of Staff of the Army, General J. Lawton Collins, conveying that he and the other ground commanders were greatly disappointed in the amount of close air support they were receiving.[95] General Collins went on to relay these sentiments to the Chief of Staff of the Air Force, General Hoyt S. Vandenberg. General Vandenberg did little to assuage the land component's concerns. Reflecting the outlook of a generation of strategic target air power advocates, he stated in a press conference that, "airplanes are inefficient weapons for killing individual soldiers."[96] He went on to state, "the best way to support the Army is to knock out the mortar before it is made. The next best is to knock it out while it is in the convoy on the way to the front. The least efficient way is to knock it out after it is already dug in."[97] Vandenberg's beliefs degraded the relationship between the air and land component even further as he pressured the air component for

---

[93] Schlight, *Help from Above*, 133 - 5.

[94] U.S. Air Force Historical Advisory Committee, *Close Air Support*, 374 - 6.

[95] Lewis, "Lt Gen Ned Almond," 55.

[96] Ibid.

[97] Ibid.

results via strategic attack and the land component began track the lack of support they were receiving.

Several post-war assessments determined there was little if any inter-service operational planning during the conflict.[98] The assessments only highlighted the 25th Infantry Division for incorporating the air component with associated requests as part of its operational planning.[99] After the war, General Almond continued his criticism of the Air Force's lack of support to the ground forces and also stated rather bluntly that the Air Force's multi-role fighter-bomber jet aircraft like the F-80, F-82, F-84, and F-86 were not suited for close air support operations; moreover, Air Force pilots were not capable of conducting close air support.[100] Like Fredendall, Almond viewed air support solely as mobile artillery for the ground forces and could not recognize the necessity for strategic attack and interdiction:

> Almost without exception fighter-bomber pilots have no conception of the extent of their overall contribution to the fire support plan in neutralizing the enemy in the pre-assault phase of an attack or in similar operations. They will not concede the great value accruing to our forces due simply to a general hammering from the air of a critical area. They cannot understand the value of what may be only the psychological effect that air support with rockets or napalm may contribute to the overall effort of our troops.[101]

The Air Force made a concerted effort following the war to emphasize the importance of air superiority and target interdiction.[102] The fact that the Air Force

---

[98] U.S. Army, "Close Air Support Issues," 42.

[99] U.S. Air Force Historical Advisory Committee, *Close Air Support*, 377.

[100] Lewis, "Lt Gen Ned Almond," 63.

[101] Ibid., 64.

[102] U.S. Air Force Historical Advisory Committee, *Close Air Support*, 179.

rendered the enemy's air power ineffective and the land component reaped the benefits of the strategic strikes was due in large part to a campaign that the ground force could never see or understand. Thus, the role of air close air support continued to be debated – the lessons from "Quesada's Air Force" forgotten. These tensions would continue to haunt air-land integration for another fifty years.

## Vietnam

The capability to fight a conventional war was waning after Korea and the ability to execute close air support at the operational level waned with it as the Air Force continued its emphasis on strategic bombing. The tactical Air Force concentrated on being multi-role, with an emphasis on strategic strike and interdiction.[103] Tactically oriented fighter pilots continued to put a high emphasis on close air support training and tactics despite the higher-level guidance to focus on strategic attack.[104]

Despite the continuing shift towards strategic attack, in 1960, the Joint Chiefs of Staff provided a definition for close air support: "Air action against hostile targets … in close proximity to friendly forces and which requires detailed integration of each air mission with the fire and movement of those forces."[105] This definition shows an evolution from Field Manual 100-20 of coequal efforts, to an integrated effort that required coordination and planning in order to be effective.

---

[103] McGrath, *Fire for Effect*, 101 – 2.

[104] C.R. Anderegg, *Sierra Hotel: Flying Air Force Fighters in the Decade after Vietnam* (Washington, D.C.: Air Force History and Museum Programs, 2001), 66.

[105] U.S. Air Force Historical Advisory Committee, *Close Air Support*, 415.

As the United States became more and more involved with the growing conflict in Southeast Asia, the employment of close air support missions grew as well. Long-range strike and interdiction missions were severely limited, as the target nomination and approval process was lengthy, protracted, rigid, and fraught with political limitations.[106] Unfortunately, close air support missions were proving ineffective as well. A 1963 study of close air support during early combat actions noted significant failings. The study asserted that the control procedures were overly cumbersome, the airspace below 9,000 feet was saturated with aircraft, and procedures were not in place to coordinate artillery with air power.[107]

By 1965, the land component had grown to battalion and brigade level operations conducting search and destroy missions that required close air support.[108] Despite operations growing and becoming more robust, overly restrictive rules of engagement hampered the process and led fighter-bomber aircraft being unable to support the ground force.[109] To overcome these issues the use of Forward Air Controllers (FAC) to coordinate, integrate, and find and fix targets, both in the air and on the ground, became indispensable. The FAC aircraft ranged from slower propeller aircraft, either the O-1, O-2, or OV-10 to the Fast FAC F-100.[110] The mission of the FAC was to integrate with the

---

[106] Ibid., 420.

[107] Ibid., 421.

[108] Ibid., 423.

[109] Ibid., 433.

[110] Schlight, *Help from Above*, 311.

land component and accomplish all of the detailed integration so that fighter-bombers could quickly and effectively employ.[111]

In 1966, the air and land component created an integrated system of baseline allocations of missions for close air support with an immediate response network capable of providing immediate close air support requests. The Tactical Air Control System (TACS) was highly effective in fulfilling emerging close air support requests. Between 1965 and 1969, the Air Force began to execute more CAS and FAC missions than any other type of mission.[112] In 1966, a study revealed that of 985 "search and destroy" land component missions, 91 percent received air support.[113] The 1967 battle for Hill 875 in Dak-To had over 2,100 close air support missions supporting the ground forces, and in the Battle of Khe Sanh the air component tasked over 25,000 sorties to provide close air support.[114] The overall commander, General William C. Westmoreland United States Military Assistance Command, Vietnam was instrumental in the overwhelming amount of close air support as he placed all air operations under a single air manager (General William W. Momyer) and directly pushed the amount of close air support he desired for the war effort.[115] General John P. McConnell United States Air Force Chief of Staff and General Harold K. Johnson United States Army Chief of Staff bolstered the air-land component relationship even further when they signed an agreement titled the "Concept for Improved Joint Air-Ground Coordination." This agreement placed all air assets under

---

[111] Ibid., 282 – 3; 317 - 9.

[112] Ibid., 306 – 8; 316.

[113] U.S. Air Force Historical Advisory Committee, *Close Air Support*, 451.

[114] Ibid., 452.

[115] Schlight, *Help from Above*, 331 - 2.

the air component commander, but decentralized execution by having the Air Support Operation Centers (aligned with land component units) task close air support missions.[116]

As the conflict matured, multi-role jet aircraft prosecuted more and more close air support sorties. Early in the conflict, the air component apportioned older A-1s, T-28s, and B-26s against close air support missions.[117] Towards the late 1960s to early 1970s F-4s, F-100s, and F-105 jet aircraft executed the preponderance of close air support missions.[118] Even the B-52 strategic bomber would prosecute CAS missions in a designation, known as Arc Light missions.[119] Of the 67,000 sorties the B-52 flew over South Vietnam, a great deal of them were supporting the land component.[120] The air component would still use single mission Forward Air Control aircraft to facilitate close air support in order to get more effects on the battlefield in less time.[121]

Close air support began to show signs of evolution during the Vietnam war. Much of the early development concerning close air support was mired by the Air Force's stubborn attachment to a doctrine centered on strategic bombing, and the Army's misunderstanding of air power's capabilities and limitations and unrealistic demands placed on the air component. From World War II to Vietnam, close air support was either executed through the will power of visionaries like Quesada and Weyland, or created by necessity by the operational environment that left close air support as the only

---

[116] U.S. Air Force, "Close Air Support Doctrine," 31 - 3.

[117] U.S. Air Force Historical Advisory Committee, *Close Air Support*, 440.

[118] Ibid., 441 – 5.

[119] Schlight, *Help from Above*, 323.

[120] Ibid., 324.

[121] Ibid., 326.

option for the air component. While air-land integration improved, and command and control procedures became more effective, the overarching lesson that many air power advocates took away from the conflict was that the air strategy was holistically ineffective because strategic attack was never given its full due. Despite these friction points, the tenets Quesada championed would gain momentum, as operations would focus more and more on Joint integration.

Close air support became more effective and was successful primarily because it was the one consistent mission during the war. Interdiction and strategic strike was sporadic at best, as the ever-changing rules of engagement and gradual response strategy did not allow for consistency. The threat environment in South Vietnam was initially permissive when executing close air support, but as either the missions moved further north or the North Vietnamese began their push to the south, the threat increased exponentially. Since close air support became the prevalent mission for the air component and the threat environment was relatively low, an expectation evolved for the land component that if close air support was required, it should immediately be available. On-call close air support was becoming the standard expectation for the land component, and that expectation still influences close air support today.

## Operation DESERT STORM

The decades leading up to Operation DESERT STORM were evolutionary and transformational. The military advanced technologically and grew in size as it attempted to out-pace its potential adversary, the Soviet Union.

During this period, the Air Force evolved its doctrine and strategy. The outcome of the Air Force's evolution was the conviction that air warfare must be unrestricted and waged at an enemy's strategic strengths. The nation prepared for near total war with the Soviet Union anticipating fighting a numerically superior enemy force. The integration between the Army and Air Force in the 1980s matured into a concept known as the Air-Land Battle.[122] The United States forecast a possible future conflict on the north German plain and through the Fulda Gap. The terrain and conditions in Eastern Europe lent itself for a decisive campaign waged with maneuver. Within that construct the land component acted as a holding force while using maneuver to attack, the air component facilitated the holding and maneuver through close air support, air interdiction attacked the rear area, and at the same time provided air superiority and suppression of enemy threat systems.[123]

In Air-Land Battle, the land component would employ aggressive maneuver to attack the opposing land force in an active defense, while the air component attacked enemy deep targets to delay and disrupt the tempo of attack. The only way to accomplish Air-Land battle was through close integration between the components. Due to that requirement, the evolution of close air support began to make substantial improvements.

The overarching goal was to achieve unity of effort between the Army and Air Force, which in turn led to the continued development of close air support. Entire networks and systems of command and control facilitated the execution of Air-Land Battle and the result was a system of orchestration and integration to counter the Soviet

---

[122] Robert Leonhard, *The Art of Maneuver: Maneuver-Warfare Theory and AirLand Battle* (Novato, CA: Predio Press, 1991), 135 – 8.

[123] Ibid., 159 – 64.

Union's overwhelming mass.[124] Fortunately, the air component had not only a significant amount of mass and depth with regard to fighter-bomber aircraft, but also ha specific mission type aircraft that carried out the required roles and functions (close air support, suppression of enemy air defenses, forward air controller, offensive/defensive counter air).

The use of single mission aircraft versus multi-role aircraft would dominate a great deal of the post-Vietnam debate, where the air force would eventually determine to procure a single mission close air support aircraft in the A-10 Thunderbolt II. The post-war shift to a single mission close air support was in part due to an agreement between the Air Force and the Army to field a single mission close air support aircraft.[125] It was also due to the Air Forces shift that a single mission aircraft was more effective than a multi-role aircraft in executing certain mission sets. However, the design of the A-10 specifically was due to threat environment experienced in Vietnam and the postulated threat of the Soviets.[126]

An example of the increasing threat environment occurred in 1971 during Operation LAM SON 719. The land component planned the operation in an area where the North Vietnamese had prepositioned over five hundred anti-aircraft-artillery pieces, ranging in size and caliber.[127] There were also several strategic and tactical level surface-to-air missiles located near the engagement area. The pre-assault fires from the fighter-

---

[124] Ibid., 165 – 86.

[125] McGrath, *Fire for Effect*, 141.

[126] Ibid., 142 – 3.

[127] Schlight, *Help from Above*, 349 - 51.

bombers and B-52s were ineffective as they attempted to deal with the surface-to-air threats.[128] As the helicopter assault force prepared for the insertion of ground forces twenty rotary wing assets were immediately shot down. Over the duration of the entire operation over 105 helicopters were lost with an additional 600 damaged.[129] Following the Vietnam conflict Soviet designed anti-air defenses would continue to become more lethal and numerous.

As the United States military doctrine continued to evolve, so did the force structure. In 1986, the Goldwater-Nichols Act brought about the most comprehensive changes to the Department of Defense since the 1947 National Security Act.[130] The Goldwater-Nichols act gave greater power and responsibility to the Chairman of the Joint Chiefs of Staff, streamlined command and control with the creation of Combatant Commands (where the Commander-in-Chief, or CINC, of those commands reported directly to the Secretary of Defense), and whose overarching premise was to promote Joint integration by quelling inter-service rivalry.[131] Included in the sweeping change was the advent of the Joint Forces Commander, whom could command the components without the constraint of coordinating with the services themselves.[132] The new command structure meant that the relationship between the Joint Forces Commander and the component commanders would be even more critical than ever. At the conclusion of

---

[128] Ibid., 350.

[129] Ibid.

[130] James R. Locher III, *Victory on the Potomac: The Goldwater-Nichols Acti Unifies the Pentagon* (College Station: Texas A&M University Press, 2007), 437 – 8.

[131] Ibid., 441. In 2002, then Secretary of Defense Donald H. Rumsfeld would direct that the term CINC should only apply to the President and Combatant Commands would be led by the title Combatant Commanders. See http://www.defense.gov/News/NewsArticle.aspx?ID=42568 (accessed 12 May 2013).

[132] Ibid.

the Cold War, the United States military was not only technologically dominant, but also massive in size.

On 2 August 1990, Iraq invaded the sovereign nation of Kuwait. In response, the United States mobilized and deployed between 575,000 and 700,000 personnel to confront the aggression. The air component alone deployed over 900 fighter-bomber aircraft to defend and repel the Iraqi military.[133]

While the coalition was bringing its forces to bear, the Iraqi military still had a significant military capability that could pose a serious threat. At the time of the conflict, it was the fourth largest army in the World. Estimates place the Iraqi army at close to 955,000 soldiers with 650,000 paramilitary forces.[134] In its inventory were an estimated 4,500 tanks, close to 500 combat aircraft, numerous surface-to-air-missiles consisting of 10 different types, and over 9,000 pieces of medium and heavy anti-aircraft-artillery.[135] General H. Norman Schwarzkopf Jr., as the Commander of United States Central Command and commander of all coalition forces during OPERATION DESERT SHIELD and OPERATION DESERT STORM, selected Air Force Lieutenant General Charles A. Horner to be the commander for U.S. and allied air operations (who was serving as the Commander of United States Central Command Air Forces at the time).[136] From the onset of preparing for hostilities there were several areas where the coalition force could have set itself up for failure, but fortunately the relationships between

---

[133] Perry D. Jamieson, *Lucrative Targets: The U.S. Air Force in the Kuwaiti Theater of Operations* (Washington, D.C.: Air Force History and Museums Program, 2001), 16.

[134] General H. Norman Schwarzkopf, *It Doesn't Take a Hero* (New York: Bantam, 1992), 348.

[135] Ibid.

[136] Ibid., 355.

Schwarzkopf and Horner, combined with the level of operational planning helped make the operation a success. Much like Bradley and Quesada, Weyland and Patton, Schwarzkopf and Horner's relationship would prove to be critical in the execution of Operation DESERT STORM.

The key to the relationship between Schwarzkopf and Horner was trust. Once selected for the position of coalition air commander, Horner conveyed to Schwarzkopf that his primary goal was to support the main effort of the land component. Horner's guarantee of unconditional air support was balanced with his role as the air expert, when it came to operational planning. In essence, Horner assured Schwarzkopf, that the Air Force would "provide CAS when and where it is needed."[137] Horner himself believed the best use of airpower was to attack strategic targets, achieve air superiority, interdict lines of communication and logistical staging areas, and to dominate enemy fielded forces.[138] These priorities were congruent with the Air-Land battle doctrine the Army and Air Force had spent the previous decades perfecting. Horner's intent was to neutralize enemy forces to such an extent that close air support would not be required.[139]

Unlike the operational air component leaders of World War II, Horner also understood the land component's need for close air support and that the Air Force had to make the necessary apportionment decisions within an adaptable, flexible framework. Very early on, Horner assured Schwarzkopf that he would receive the necessary amount of close air support through a push CAS system, where aircraft were assigned to

---

[137] Tom Clancy with General Chuck Horner, *Every Man a Tiger:  The Gulf War Campaign* (New York: Penguin Putnam Inc., 1999), 21; 244 – 5; 247 – 8.

[138] Ibid., 244.

[139] Ibid., 246.

dedicated close air support missions. Horner directed the Joint Planning Team to devise a command and control system that could rapidly task or re-task air missions to support the land component.[140]

The operational plan was for the system to ensure enough close air support was available when needed, but to not waste missions that could be tasked against operational and strategic target sets. Again, like Quesada in World War II, Horner was able to build a relationship with Schwarzkopf through trust and his commander's intent to support the land component. The combination of Horner's priorities with the trust he built with Schwarzkopf created a foundation for success in the campaign. This allowed Horner to focus on the necessary strategic targets while still providing the land component with the necessary support.

Even though Horner had an excellent relationship with Schwarzkopf and his commander priorities supported the operational ends, certain elements in the Air Force clung to the dogmatic doctrine that air power alone could achieve victory. While Horner was in Riyadh making plans for the overall campaign as part of Central Command, the Air Force tapped Colonel John A. Warden III to begin building a strategic air campaign to support Operation DESERT STORM.[141] Much like Mitchell, Spaatz, and Doolittle, Warden saw the air component as primarily a strategic bombing and interdiction force in the operation. Warden's plan theorized that the most effective way to achieve victory was through an air line of effort that prioritized attacking binned targets focusing

---

[140] Ibid., 245.

[141] Richard T. Reynolds, *Heart of the Storm: The Genesis of the Air Campaign Against Iraq* (Maxwell Air Force Base, AL: Air University Press, 1997), 120 – 2.

primarily on Iraqi leadership, production centers, infrastructure, the population's support, and lastly the military.[142] His theory posited that by waging the air component against the correct targets, it would not be necessary to attack the fielded forces and close air support could even be detrimental to the effort. Close air support should only act as an operational reserve for the land component.[143]

There in essence became two planning efforts by two Joint Planning Teams, one in Riyadh and one in Washington D.C. In Riyadh, Horner was integrating close air support as an integral part of the ground component decisive maneuver. In Washington Warden was creating a separate campaign for the Air Force ignoring the ground component completely. As Warden briefed his concept to Horner in Riyadh, Horner asked Warden about the plan for the enemy fielded forces.[144] Warden's response was that the fielded forces would not require attack after his strategic air campaign and allocating air power against them could actually be a detriment to the operation.[145] That was the end of Warden's plan. Horner rejected Warden's approach because his design would not support the operation. Horner's team planned its air campaign to achieve the necessary effects in order to synchronize its support of the land component.[146] Once the coalition ground campaign began, many of the air assets that were initially supporting

---

[142] Ibid., 135.

[143] John A. Warden III, *The Air Campaign: Planning for Combat* (Lincoln, NE: iUniverse, 2000), 89.

[144] Reynolds, *Heart of the Storm*, 150 – 2.

[145] Ibid., 155.

[146] Clancy and Horner, *Every Man a Tiger*, 261 – 5.

strategic attack and air superiority began supporting the land component through interdiction and close air support.[147]

The execution of Operation DESERT STORM was an operational success. The air campaign began on 17 January 1991; the initial stages of the operation struck strategic targets, air defense networks, and fielded forces.[148] The Iraqi ground forces withstood near continuous air attack for thirty-eight days in preparation for the coalition ground attack.[149] As the air campaign began to achieve its effect on the long-range strike targets, the ground campaign commenced and the air component began allocating almost all of its missions towards shaping the battlefield. On 11 February 1991 for example, of the 986 strike missions, the air component tasked 933 missions to support ground unit operations.[150] The full weight of the ground invasion lasted four days with over 900 fighter-bomber aircraft.[151] The operation resembled Vietnam in size only, as the air component finally struck the proper balance between close air support and long-range strike. The close relationship between Schwarzkopf and Horner was noticeable to not only those in uniform, but also to the public, as Horner received as much praise, publicity and accolades as did Schwarzkopf.

---

[147] Ibid., 343 – 5. Unfortunately, following the war, Warden's thoughts on airpower would gain a substantial following and due to the success of Operation DESERT STORM, some would view the results of the air campaign as a validation of his theory.

[148] Jamieson, *Lucrative Targets*, 41 – 3.

[149] Ibid., 83 – 5.

[150] Clancy and Horner, *EveryMan a Tiger*, 467.

[151] Jamieson, *Lucrative Targets*, 16.

While the operation was a resounding success, there were still points to give the United States military pause. For the first time since World War II, the United States Air Force had to plan and conduct operations with an active air defense--the coalition lost thirty-nine fixed wing aircraft and five helicopters. Many of these losses were attributed to SAMs and AAA, as the air component struck targets deeper in Iraqi territory and the Iraqi mobile defenses moved further to the South.[152] While the air component had long trained to deal with a robust Soviet anti-air threat, the proliferation of those threats to other countries was seen in Iraq.

It is important to note that the coalition had time to build up their forces in anticipation for attack. The air component had not only a great deal of depth, but also an

---

[152] Jamieson, *Lucrative Targets*, 92 – 7.

41

extensive number of specialized aircraft for all mission sets. The air threat, while significant at the time, was neutralized rather quickly to allow support to ground force's maneuver. In retrospect, the operation turned out to be less joint than expected. The air component had the benefit of having several weeks to shape the battlefield in preparation for the land component. Thus, the Air Force got what it wanted through the phasing of the campaign, making an easy transition from one mission to the next to satisfy the land component.

## Operation ENDURING FREEDOM

On September 11, 2001, following the attack on the World Trade Center and Pentagon, the United States leadership determined that the Al Qaeda terrorist network and supporting Taliban support posed a threat to national security. In order to show decisive action, beginning on 7 October 2011 B-1, B-2, B-52, and Naval F-14 and F/A-18 fighter-bomber aircraft began attacking the country of Afghanistan's antiquated integrated air defense systems and terrorist training camps with the support of special forces and other governmental agencies.[153] As the operation continued to evolve, the coalition led effort began to grow and more aggressively execute offensive operations against Al Qaeda and Taliban forces.[154]

The operational environment surrounding Operation ENDURING FREEDOM (OEF) was significantly different from any other major operation for the Joint force.

---

[153] Lester W. Grau and Dodge Billingsley, *Operation ANACONDA: America's First Major Battle in Afghanistan* (Lawrence, KS: University Press of Kansas, 2011), 47 – 9.

[154] Ibid., 85 – 96.

There was not a defined forward edge of the battle area, or a defined enemy or friendly held geographical area. From the beginning of the campaign, air and special operations forces were linked together in a devastating pairing that proved overwhelmingly effective.[155] After several months of special operations supported by the air component, the coalition force planned a major operation in which several key factors presented themselves with regard to close air support operations.

Operation ANACONDA, from 2 March 2002 to 16 March 2002, was one of the first large combat operations that took place.[156] With the arrival of conventional land forces came traditional ground force paradigms from 1942; the conventional force believed that air power served only as mobile artillery, and all of the assets should fall under the authority of Joint Forces Land Component Commander. The operation highlighted several recurring friction points between air and land component doctrines, relationships, and operational planning.

The objective of ANACONDA was to clear the Khowst-Gardez valley of Al Qaeda and Taliban forces.[157] The earliest elements of operational planning began in January 2002, but did not fully evolve until February.[158] On 17 February, the joint planning team briefed the CFLCC, Lieutenant General Paul T. Mikolashek, United States Army, the major components of the operational plan (as well as Major General Franklin

---

[155] Steve Call, *Danger Close: Tactical Air Controllers in Afghanistan and Iraq* (College Station: Texas A&M University Press, 2007), 25 – 41.

[156] Grau and Billingsley, *Operation ANACONDA,* 1 - 2.

[157] U.S. Air Force, "Operation ANACONDA An Air Power Perspective" (Washington, D.C.: Headquarters Air Force AF/XOL, 7 February 2005), 21 – 3.

[158] Ibid.

L. Hagenbeck, United States Army, the CFLCC-Forward).[159] The chain of command and unity of command was extremely disjointed. The 10th Mountain Division lacked an air planning cell. The special operations, command elements, air component, and planning teams were spread across several locations.[160] Ultimately, this led to a lack of integration not only between the operational leaders themselves but also between the operational leaders and the planning team. The joint planning team (JPT) published the operations order (OPORD) on 20 February 2002, which detailed the course of action and concept for operations.[161] While early intelligence estimates incorrectly estimated the enemy disposition between 168 and 1,000, one of the more critical key factors that led to failure was the lack of joint planning between the air and land component.[162]

The JPT had constructed a baseline request for close air support sorties in line with an apportionment model, but the CFACC, Lieutenant General T. Michael Mosely, United States Air Force, did not learn of the operation until 23 February 2002, only five days prior to the execution of the operation.[163] Consequently, the JPT failed to account for command and control for CAS requests, pre-assault fires from the air component, and supporting requirements for close air support.[164] The CFACC estimated that he could provide "two simultaneous CAS events," without a firm understanding of the necessary

---

[159] Ibid., 24 – 5.

[160] Sean Naylor, *Not a Good Day to Die: The Untold Story of Operation ANACONDA* (New York: The Penguin Group, 2005), 134 – 5.

[161] U.S. Air Force, "Operation ANACONDA," 21 – 3.

[162] Ibid., 23.

[163] Naylor, *Not a Good Day*, 136 – 7.

[164] Ibid., 136.

support, fires deconfliction, or land component scheme of maneuver.[165] The conventional land component devolved the relationships and support structure the special operations forces had developed into an ineffective and unsupportable approach.

The operation began on 2 March and immediately, calls for close air support became overwhelming.[166] The ground maneuver plan had broken down, leaving the 101st as a blocking force. Now exposed on the landing zone they came under effective fire from multiple hidden locations.[167] Lacking a coherent structure that allowed unity of command, the operation quickly became chaotic as fog and friction exerted its influence. Within the first 72 hours of the operation, the air component employed over 750 bombs executing close air support.[168] By 4 March 2002, the coalition began to lose momentum, as the enemy forces held the high ground. The air components weapons effects were for the most part ineffective as fighter-bomber aircraft attempted to target small caves or bunkers they could not see from high altitude, use precision guided munitions with inaccurate source data, or joint direct attack munitions against mobile targets.[169]

As the CFACC surged to meet the CFLCC's request for air support, aircraft came dangerously close to having a mid-air collision with other aircraft or bombing friendly forces on the ground as deconfliction, command and control, and integration degraded.[170] The coalition was eventually able to regain the offensive and clear the remaining portions

[165] U.S. Air Force, "Operation ANACONDA," 21 – 3.

[166] Call, *Danger Close,* 66 – 8.

[167] Malcolm MacPherson, *Roberts Ridge: A Story of Courage and Sacrifice on Takur Ghar Mountain, Afghanistan* (New York: Bantam Dell, 2005), 74 – 6.

[168] U.S. Air Force, "Operation ANACONDA," 69 - 71.

[169] Grau and Billingsley, *Operation ANACONDA,* 231 – 80.

[170] Ibid., 273 – 4.

of the valley, but the operation highlighted two overarching key factors, a failure of unity of effort between the CFLCC and CFACC and the lack of detailed planning at the operational level. Close air support again devolved to 1942 era tenets. The operational leaders did not have a relationship that ensured their priorities and objectives were aligned and did not have a shared understanding concerning the employment of close air support. As a result, the joint planning team was incomplete and did not create a comprehensive and detailed plan for close air support.

Following the operation, General Hagenbeck was critical of the air support he received from the CFACC, but he did not accept responsibility for the operation being planned without a unity of effort required for joint operations.[171] The various components supporting the operation all had major headquarters staffs and functions dispersed throughout the area of responsibility (AOR).[172] ANACONDA called for special operations to work with conventional land component forces, Afghanistan forces, and coalition forces in a non-linear battlespace and integrated plan.[173] A major shift in operations for any campaign of this magnitude requires detailed planning and coordination for successful integration.

The haphazard planning, incomplete lash up of several components, and the late inclusion of the air component led to the air liaisons having to piece together a hasty airspace control plan. The land component was also worried about losing the element of surprise due to pre-assault fires, and therefore planned for air power to shape the

---

[171] Call, *Danger Close,* 74 - 5.

[172] U.S. Air Force, "Operations ANACONDA," 24.

[173] Ibid., 33.

battlespace as late as possible prior to maneuvering land forces to the objective area. That combined with confusing rules of engagement, poor intelligence, and lack of poor commander and planning team relationships led to minimal pre-assault fires.[174] The result of the suboptimal planning led to ineffective execution during the operation, the same problems that plagued the Meuse-Argonne in 1918, Operation TORCH in 1942, and Korea in 1952.

Once the operation began, the incongruent planning process began to manifest itself immediately. The pre-assault fires from the air component came dangerously close to a ground team, who were unaware that the strikes were supposed to take place. As a result, they called for the fighters and bombers to cease their strikes.[175] There was not a comprehensive command and control to facilitate adaptation to the changing plan for the air component.[176] The enemy quickly gained the offensive during the initial stages exploiting the seams between the various forces and securing the high ground to attack the coalition. Due to the confusing and complicated plan, an AC-130 lost situational awareness and inadvertently fired on friendly forces, killing one U.S. soldier.[177] With a lack of robust command and control, and deconfliction degraded, air power became ineffective as the proper assets were not available and aircraft felt they could not safely employ for fear of hitting friendly forces.[178]

---

[174] Ibid., 37 – 41; 56 – 7.

[175] Grau and Billingsley, *Operation ANACONDA,* 183 - 5.

[176] U.S. Air Force, "Operation ANACONDA," 50 - 4.

[177] Naylor, *Not a Good Day,* 205.

[178] Grau and Billingsley, *Operation ANACONDA,* 273 - 4.

Beginning with the lack of a relationship between the air and land component, the air component did not have the trust that they could safely employ, and the land component did not trust the air component to affect the battlefield unless the situation was dire. The detailed integration required for successful close air support was not present. The operational plan also had difficult rules of engagement concerning who had the authority for clearing air strikes that led to lengthy delays in providing close air support due to the disjointed command structure.[179]

The situation became reminiscent of the Vietnam conflict where close air support was the primary mission for the air component and a technologically superior force was pitted against an elusive enemy who possessed an unsurpassed familiarity with the terrain and environment. Unfortunately, the result of Operation ANACONDA was eerily similar to Korea where a conventional land component was ineffectively integrated with the air component and was unable to achieve their desired objectives. The poor relationships between the ground commander and air power leadership showed the same strains between Almond and Weyland. The result of the inadequate operational planning, lack of relationship between operational leaders, and multi-vectored lanes of effort, was that tactical execution had to overcome operational shortcomings in order to prevail.

Operation ANACONDA is a cautionary tale; the mistakes of this planning will be magnified for a JPT and leaders for a future conflict facing an A2/AD environment. The JPT was not integrated, lacked commander interaction, did not have a shared set of priorities, had differing perspectives on how the joint force would integrate, and as a

---

[179] U.S. Air Force, "Operation ANACONDA," 40.

result was a near disaster and a less than decisive outcome. Within ANACONDA, two equally sized land components faced each other in an environment that held no external threat to the air component. There was a mix of single mission close air support assets with multi-role fighter-bombers available for close air support, but as the tactical situation on the ground devolved, capabilities ceased to matter in order to get effects on the battlespace. Even with an evenly numerically matched land component and threat free air domain, there was a considerable amount of risk to the coalition force. The lack of planning and disjointed leadership left a dangerous gap. Fortunately, following Operation ANACONDA the leadership placed a high emphasis on joint training, close air support, and joint doctrine. That emphasis would pay dividends as the operational planning began for Operation IRAQI FREEDOM.

## Operation IRAQI FREEDOM

While there is significant debate concerning the road to war and the strategic decisions concerning Operation IRAQI FREEDOM (OIF), operationally the integration between the land and the air component was relatively successful. The success of Phases I, II, and III operations during OIF was due in large part to the military's focus on joint doctrine and training that resulted in trust, familiarization, and the first true joint venture by the military. While the coalition failed to adequately plan for Phase IV and V operations, the close air support planning for Phase II and III integrated the joint force effectively. OIF took the lessons from Operation DESERT STORM, OEF, and other previous campaigns and applied them in such a fashion as to quickly gain and maintain the offensive against the Iraqi military force.

In the months leading up to OIF, a series of planning sessions devised a campaign that integrated a Marine Corps sector, Army sector, and special operations missions into a comprehensive operational plan.[180] The plan's operational approach was to achieve quick and decisive effects through simultaneity against strategic, operational, and tactical targets. The overarching objective was to attack the regime and associated command and control while maneuvering to secure Baghdad as quickly as possible.[181] The numerous operational objectives relevant to Phases II and III operations were to defeat or compel capitulation of Iraqi forces, neutralize regime leadership, neutralize Iraqi theater ballistic missiles (TBM)/weapons of mass destruction (WMD) delivery systems, control WMD structure, ensure territorial integrity of Iraq, neutralize Iraqi regime's command and control and security forces, gain and maintain air, maritime, and space supremacy.[182] In order to accomplish these effects and objectives the air component would execute long-range strike, interdiction, and close air support simultaneously to facilitate the land components thrust towards the capitol.[183] Despite years of sanctions and adverse actions during Operation SOUTHERN WATCH (OSW), the Iraqi military still possessed a capable air defense network. Estimates placed the Iraqi integrated air defenses (IADS) close to 210 SAMs, 150 early warning radars, and thousands of AAA pieces.[184] Even with the robust threat, the coalition only lost one fixed wing aircraft and six attack

---

[180] Williamson Murray and Robert H. Scales, Jr., *The Iraq War: A Military History* (Cambridge, MA: Harvard University Press, 2005), 59 - 71.

[181] Tommy Franks and Malcolm McConnell, *American Soldier* (New York: Regan Books, 2004), 338 - 41.

[182] U.S. Air Force, "Operation IRAQI FREEDOM" (Washington, D.C.: Headquarters U.S. Air Force Assessment and Analysis Division: 30 April 2003), 4.

[183] Murray and Scales, *The Iraq War*, 171 - 5.

[184] U.S. Air Force, "Operation IRAQI FREEDOM," 3.

helicopters due to enemy fire.[185]  In contrast to Operation DESERT STORM, Operation

IRAQI FREEDOM planned for minimal time between an initial air campaign and the

ground invasion.  Between 19 March 2003 and 10 April 2003, the joint force was able to

achieve near simultaneity between the air and land forces and by doing so reached the

apogee of close air support.  To execute a combined air campaign and ground force

maneuver, the air and land components needed to work together to balance priorities in

attacking strategic targets and providing close air support. [186]  Within its execution, the

CFACC apportioned over 50 percent of its missions towards close air support attacking

over 17,500 targets in support of ground forces.[187]  By component, the United States Air

Force utilized 344 fighter-bombers, the United States Marine Corps used 130 fighters,

and the United States Navy used 232 fighters to support the campaign.[188]  The air

campaign finished major combat operations on 14 April 2003 and continued to provide

close air support until 18 December 2011.[189]  The successfulness of the air and land

integration is due in large part to the planning for close air support by the JPT and the

relationship between the CFLCC and the CFACC during execution.

A key factor that led to the successful integration of the air and land component

was the overall operational art the air component operational leaders presented to the

JPTs.  During planning the commander's intent for close air support was that the air

component would take any action or risk to protect ground forces through the execution

---

[185] Ibid.

[186] Franks and McConnell, *American Soldier,* 382 - 3.

[187] U.S. Air Force, "Operation IRAQI FREEDOM," 5.

[188] Ibid., 6.

[189] Ibid., 15.

of close air support.[190] Lessons learned from OEF and Operation DESERT STORM were incorporated into the joint planning for OIF. Even though the plan called for different sectors, supported by different components, with different missions (a special operations sector, an Army Sector, a Marine sector), close air support was the integrator that tied them all together.

The JPT constructed an air support plan that facilitated not only attacking long-range strike targets but also the land component. The initial concept for the airspace control plan allowed the air component to shift from interdiction to close air support. In execution however, the placement of the fire support coordination line (FSCL) placed a heavy burden upon the land component air liaison for approving interdiction requests that were short of the FSCL, which due to the extended range of artillery and rockets extended for miles past the friendly forward line of troops (FLOT).[191]

It can be asserted that the FSCL had become an outdated fire support coordination measure left over from Air-Land Battle doctrine. Due to increased surface-to-surface fire ranges, the FSCL became overly restrictive and constrained the air component's ability to affect the battlefield within the 3d Division sector.[192] Within the Marine sector, the operational planners remedied the situation with the creation of the battlefield coordination line (BCL), so targets short of the FSCL but long of the BCL required

---

[190] Murray and Scales, *The Iraq War*, 173.

[191] Author's personal experience as a Close Air Support planner and Strike Package Mission Commander during Operation IRAQI FREEDOM.

[192] Rebecca Grant, "Marine Air in the Mainstream," *Air Force Magazine*, June 2004, http://www.airforcemag.com/MagazineArchive/Pages/2004/June%202004/0604marine.aspx (accessed 24 April 2013).

minimal coordination to attack.[193] The air component adapted a process to expedite the request chain by using streamlined "kill-containers" to make the process more effective in order to overcome the Army sector's burdensome procedures.[194] Those friction points aside, the key factor that should be carried forward is the JPT designed a plan with a detailed framework that could be adapted once in execution. With that framework in place, simplicity and adaptability made the joint force more effective.

A key factor between the CFACC and CFLCC relationship came during a period of intense sand storms from 25 March 2003 until 27 March 2003 that made air support virtually impossible. During these storms, the CFACC, Lieutenant General T. Michael Moseley, communicated to the CFLCC, Lieutenant General David D. McKiernan United States Army, that it would be extremely difficult to support the ensuing land component maneuver due to the loss of visibility.[195] The air component and land component working together adapted the plan where the land force would execute an operational pause until the storms passed. During the pause, the air component would continue to attack static targets from assets that could deliver weapons through the weather.[196] The adaptability and compromise between the two components were critical elements of the relationship between the CFLCC and CFACC.

There are some considerations to keep in mind when reflecting upon OIF. Due to the fear of regime collapse and the Joint Forces Commander's operational approach that

---

[193] Ibid.

[194] Murray and H. Scales, *The Iraq War*, 169 - 72.

[195] Franks and McConnell, *American Soldier*, 501 - 7.

[196] Ibid., 502 – 3.

focused on speed and decisiveness, the land and air component commenced operations simultaneously. This prevented the air component from ensuring air supremacy prior to the land component's maneuver. The air components inability to guarantee air supremacy is offset with the fact that several years of Operation SOUTHERN and NORTHERN WATCH combined with economic sanctions had a considerably degraded Iraqi air defenses. Finally, while a smaller air component prosecuted OIF than DESERT STORM, the air component still had an overwhelming numerical advantage against the Iraqi military. These considerations are important to carry forward as the military transitions to a new operational environment.

## 2004 To Present

Following major combat operations in OIF and throughout OEF, close air support has come to resemble the Vietnam conflict again with tendencies from 1942. There is no threat to fighter-bomber aircraft, close air support is the primary mission for fires, and there is unrestricted access to the battlefield. The land component has come to expect continuous coverage from close air support assets without any gaps in coverage and the air component has become accustomed to little preparation or planning in support of most emerging close air support requests. There have been excellent examples of operational leadership within the components as leaders have formed bonds and relationships to ensure the joint force meets its operational objectives. For example, while serving as commander United States Air Forces Central Command, then Lieutenant General Gilmary Michael Hostage III assured General Stanley A. McChrystal (followed by General David H. Petraeus), who was commanding Multi-National Force Iraq, that the air component would always support the needs and requirements of the land component with all available assets.[197]

The presented historical themes have ranged from periods where the use of close air support has been either eschewed or ineffective to periods where the land and air components effectively integrated to provide a synergistic effect. During the periods where the ground and air forces have not been in alignment, it has been due to the joint planning team's inability to plan the utilization and prioritization of close air support. A smaller force size and greater threat will only increase the consequences for short falls in planning. Conversely, when close air support has been effective, there have been key factors that have been consistent throughout the integration of land and air power. Therefore, the joint planning team should focus on these key factors when operationally planning close air support. Those key factors include significant joint principles, elements of operational design, and joint functions (see Figure 1).

While the joint planning team is critical, of even more importance is the relationship between the joint force commander, the joint force land component commander, and the joint force air component commander. History again has shown that when the land and air components are at odds with their priorities, there is a resultant negative effect upon the entire operation. When the JFLCC and JFACC priorities are in alignment and there is a mutually beneficial relationship, the joint force is successful. Therefore it is critical that the land/air leadership team focus on a shared intent with trust,

---

[197] Mark V. Schanz, "Committing everyting to the battlefield," *Air Force Magazine*, July 2011, http://www.airforcemag.com/MagazineArchive/Pages/2011/July%202011/0711battlefield.aspx (accessed 11 November 2012).

proper prioritization, while accepting minor mission degradation for greater integration (Figure1).

In order to be successful, operational leaders and the joint planning team must carry forward the key tenets of successfulness for close air support. Unfortunately, as operations begin to drawdown in Southwest Asia, the focus on the Pacific Theater gains momentum, the force size shrinks, and there is a doctrinal effort for a more air-sea centric campaign in an A2/AD environment, the joint force risks relapsing into dangerous historical habit patterns. The joint force can ill afford to fall into the same paradigm of 1918, 1942, 1950, and so on if does not employ specific key tenets of operational planning and leadership. Unless a concerted effort is made to embody these key factors now, history may again repeat itself.

```
┌─────────────────────────────┐   ┌─────────────────────────────┐
│        OPERATIONAL          │   │        OPERATIONAL          │
│                             │   │                             │
│   PLANNING KEY FACTORS      │   │   LEADER KEY FACTORS        │
│                             │   │                             │
│  • Joint Principles         │   │  • Intent and trust         │
│                             │   │                             │
│     o  Mass                 │   │  • Prioritization           │
│                             │   │                             │
│     o  Maneuver             │   │  • Minor mission degradation │
│                             │   │                             │
│     o  Offensive            │   │     for greater integration │
│                             │   └─────────────────────────────┘
│     o  Simplicity           │
│                             │
│  • Elements of Operational  │
│                             │
│  Design                     │
│                             │
│     o  Center of Gravity    │
│                             │
│     o  Decisive Point       │
│                             │
│     o  Anticipation         │
│                             │
│  • Joint Functions          │
│                             │
│     o  Command and          │
│                             │
│        Control              │
│                             │
│     o  Movement and         │
│                             │
│        Maneuver             │
│                             │
│     o  Fires                │
│                             │
│     o  Intelligence         │
│                             │
└─────────────────────────────┘
```

**Figure 1. Key Factors of Operational Planning and Leadership**

# CHAPTER 3:  JOINT CLOSE AIR SUPPORT PLANNING CONSIDERATIONS

In contrast to the historical analysis presented in the previous chapter, today's air component is smaller, multi-role, and has the potential to operate in a much more robust anti-air threat environment.  In an ideal situation, the JPT would arrange operations in such a fashion that the air component achieves air superiority prior to the commencement of a ground campaign with close air support.[1]  While it may be ideal to shape the battle-space, the land component may not be able to wait several days for an air campaign to have an effect, leaving the land and air component to conduct close air support in a high threat environment.  The need for a simultaneous air and land engagement may be due to regime collapse, national instability, the need to rapidly impact a center of gravity, the requirement to secure Weapons of Mass Destruction (WMD), or a myriad of other reasons.  Recent campaigns have exhibited simultaneity with regard to the air component's execution and the land component's departure.  In the same respect the land component may have become accustomed to persistent close air support and intelligence, surveillance, and reconnaissance (ISR) support that is no longer feasible in an A2/AD, force constrained scenario.

In order to be successful, joint planning teams will need to account for the operational environment and diligently construct a plan that maximizes the integration between the land and air component.  Mere apportionment and allocation will not be enough to be successfully conduct close air support in this new environment.  Future

---

[1] U.S. Air Force, *Air Force Doctrine Document 1:  Air Force Basic Doctrine, Organization, and Command* (Washington, D.C.:  U.S. Air Force, 14 October 2011), 19.

campaigns will require a Joint Operational Planning Process (JOPP) that integrates the close air support within the operational art and operational design in order to be successful.[2]

Once JOPP has begun, the foundation for an effective joint campaign is the relationship between the JTF Commander and the component commanders.[3] A synergistic relationship will ensure the commander's operational art conveys the critical interconnectedness of the air and land components to conduct close air support. When plan initiation has commenced and the JPT begins their mission analysis, the Joint Intelligence Preparation of the Operational Environment (JIPOE) should highlight the capabilities of an A2/AD environment and frame the need for employing key considerations in order to be successful.[4] The combination of an A2/AD environment with the allocated forces from the Global Force Management Implementation Guidance (GFMIG) should highlight the need for detailed integration between the ground force and the air forces as the JPT enters operational design.[5] As the JPT continues the planning process and identifies the military end states, termination, centers of gravity, objectives, decisive points, effects, and tasks, the requirement for close air support should begin to present itself.[6] The JPT should then construct lines of effort with supporting intermediate factors and effects that take into account the requirements for JCAS in a high threat

---

[2] U.S. Joint Chiefs of Staff, *Joint Operation Planning*, Joint Publication 5-0 (Washington, D.C.: Joint Chiefs of Staff, 11 August 2011), I-5.

[3] Ibid.

[4] Ibid., III-9.

[5] Ibid., I-3.

[6] Ibid., H-1.

environment in order to begin course of action (COA) development.[7]  It is critical the JPT recognize the following key factors in order to ensure success.

## Joint Principles

The JPT will need to consider several key joint principles to facilitate close air support.  The following joint principles have always been important to joint operations, but they will take on an increased level of criticalness in the future operational environment.  The first Joint principle to address is **Mass**.

> The purpose of mass is to concentrate the effects of combat power at the most advantageous place and time to produce decisive results.  In order to achieve mass, appropriate joint force capabilities are integrated and synchronized where they will have a decisive effect in a short period of time.  Mass often must be sustained to have the desire effect.  Massing effect of combat power, rather than concentrating forces, can enable even numerically inferior forces to produce decisive results and minimize human losses and waste of resources.[8]

In a future, resource constrained environment, the air component will utilize multi-role assets against a variety of mission sets and targets.  The ability to mass will take a concerted effort with such a limited force.  Colonel John Warden posited that allocating air assets for close air support detracts from the overall effect of a "strategic air campaign."[9]  He went on state that JCAS should only be used as an "operational

---

[7] Ibid., I-5.

[8] U.S. Joint Chiefs of Staff, *Joint Operations,* Joint Publication 3-0  (Washington, D.C.:  Joint Chiefs of Staff, 11 August 2011), A-2.

[9] Warden, *The Air Campaign*, 88.

reserve."[10] In the future conflicts, there is some utility to this line of logic. The air component will need to mass its limited force against long-range strike targets in order to achieve an effect, but it will also need to mass those same assets in support of the land component; but not only as an operational reserve, it will need to be synchronized as a coordinated main effort.

The JPT will need to arrange joint operations such that the air component shifts from strategic attack and interdiction to mass at the appropriate time to support the land component as it moves to an objective or decisive point. Due to the smaller force size and the nature of the threat environment aircraft will be unable to loiter over the battlefield to provide persistent support. There will be greater periods between individual attacks as aircraft hold at increased distances from the enemy threats. In order to achieve the desired effects more aircraft will have to mass to support close air support. Apportioning a percentage of the force will be inadequate. The JPT must identify key engagement areas and decisive points to mass the land and air component against together.

The next Joint principle is **Maneuver**.

The purpose of maneuver is to place the enemy in a position of disadvantage through the flexible application of combat power. Maneuver is the movement of forces in relation to the enemy to secure positional advantage, usually in order to deliver – or threaten delivery of- the direct and indirect fires of the maneuvering force. Effective maneuver keeps the enemy off balance and thus also protects the friendly force. It contributes materially in exploiting success, preserving freedom of action, and reducing vulnerability by continually posing new problems for the enemy.[11]

---

[10] Ibid., 89.

[11] U.S. Joint Chiefs of Staff, *Joint Operations*, A-2.

Maneuver has always been a critical component of close air support but within the A2/AD environment, the JPT will need to plan its use in a more proactive manner. Historically, liaison elements with the land component would determine the use for close air support within the ground forces scheme of maneuver. Aircrew would then learn of their intended use upon checking in with the ground force. Due to the increased threat and limited force size operational planners will need to construct a framework for the integration of the air and land components use of maneuver. Within the concept of operations and operational plan, a framework will need to convey how the air component will mass and which elements are responsible for holding the enemy, interdicting the rear area, and the comprehensive fires integration in order to gain an advantage. Operational planning of maneuver cannot be left to just assigning an asset as part of the fires plan. A more rigorous design of supporting fires and areas of responsibility is necessary to achieve the required effects.

The next Joint principle is **Offensive**.

> The purpose of an offensive action is to seize, retain, and exploit the initiative. Offensive action is the most effective and decisive way to achieve a clearly defined objective. Offensive operations are the means by which a military force seizes and holds the initiative while maintaining freedom of action and achieving decisive results. The importance of offensive action is fundamentally true across all levels of war. Commanders adopt the defensive only as a temporary expedient and must seek every opportunity to seize or regain the initiative. An offensive spirit must be in conduct of all defensive operations.[12]

---

[12] Ibid., A-1.

The JPT must construct an operational plan that exploits the offensive while being adaptable enough to transition to defensive operations. Forecasting that the land and air component will commence operations simultaneously, the JPT must anticipate when the air component will need to shift from long-range strike to close air support for the land component. These transitions are critical in gaining and maintaining the offensive.

In order to facilitate achieving the offensive the JPT should identify decisive points and potential engagement areas where close air support is critical.[13] Early identification of engagement areas by the JPT will allow the air component to anticipate and prepare for close air support operations (which will be essential in a contested environment). Engagement areas will also allow the air component to transition from long-range strike to interdiction to close air support as friendly and enemy forces come closer to reaching the predesigned engagement areas. This will ensure the joint force is able to mass and maneuver appropriately. If the land component makes contact with the enemy prior to an engagement area or decisive point in a meeting engagement, the operational plan must have the flexibility to facilitate the air component shifting from long-range strike and air superiority to a comprehensive close air support effort. Due to the limited size of both components, quickly regaining the offensive is crucial, and the air component must surge to achieve that effect.

The final Joint principle is **Simplicity**.

> The purpose of simplicity is to increase the probability that plans and operations will be executed as intended by preparing clear, uncomplicated plans and concise orders. Simplicity contributes to successful operations. Simple plans and clear concise orders minimize misunderstandings and

---

[13] Ibid., III-28.

confusion. When other factors are equal, the simplest plan is preferable. Simplicity in plans allows better understanding and executing planning at all echelons. Simplicity and clarity of expression greatly facilitate mission execution in the stress, fatigue, fog of war, and complexities of modern combat, and are especially critical to success in multinational operations.[14]

The nature of the A2/AD environment will increase the complexity of operations. The operational construct the JPT utilizes to support integrating the land and air component must be simple enough to execute under intense fire. Simplicity should also translate into adaptability. Operating within a robust threat environment with a limited force means that the air and land component must be able to adapt a simple plan in order to negate the enemies input into the system. The air component should be able to shift from long-range strike to interdiction and close air support rapidly in a simplified system of command and control. Likewise, the land component should be able to synchronize their maneuver to decisive points and engagement areas to ensure they have the required air support. An overly complicated and intricate plan dependent upon multiple assumptions and linkages will adversely affect the operational plans integration of the land and air component.

Tying the joint principles to close air support within a comprehensive campaign plan is essential for effective close air support role in operational planning. The JPT will then use the operational elements of design and joint functions to integrate the land component and the air component in order to meet the operational plan's (OPLAN) termination criteria and military end state.[15]

---

[14] Ibid., A-3.

[15] U.S. Joint Chiefs of Staff, *Joint Operation Planning*, III-19.

## Elements of Operational Design

Within the elements of operational design, there are key factors the JPG must be cognizant of for successful close air support in an A2/AD environment. Those key factors include the center of gravity (COG), objectives, decisive points, effects, direct/indirect approach, anticipation, arranging operations, and forces and functions.[16] The use of these key factors within operational design will allow the JPT to highlight critical linkages within the OPLAN where close air support is necessary. These highlights and linkages will ensure integration between the land and air component so the joint force can meet their objectives. Again, in the past when the air component had a larger force and there was a smaller air threat, an effective apportionment model may have sufficed for operational planning. In an environment with a higher threat and smaller force, the JPT will need a greater effort in planning in order to ensure success. The first step the JPT will need to accomplish is to determine whether close air support is critical in effecting the center of gravity.

According to Joint Publication 5-0, *Joint Operation Planning*, "A center of gravity is a source of power that provides moral or physical strength, freedom of action, or will to act."[17] Joint Publication 5-0 goes on to state that "at the operational level, a COG often is associated with the adversary's military capabilities – such as a powerful element of the armed forces – but could include other capabilities in the operational

---

[16] Ibid., III-18.
[17] Ibid., III-22.

environment."[18] When the JPT determines the enemy's operational COG, it will also determine the other factors that affect the COG through COG analysis (the critical capabilities, critical requirements, critical vulnerabilities to the COG, and the objectives, decisive points, effects, and direct or indirect approach to the COG).[19] Once the JPT begins course of action (COA) development it should determine whether close air support would be a key enabler for the air and land component in exerting the necessary power against the COG. Historically, especially within recent conflicts, while the JPT has identified the enemy force as the operational center of gravity, the air component has influenced the COG via an indirect approach with long-range strikes against critical vulnerabilities and requirements, and the land component has attacked the COG directly with only a portion of the air component supporting it.

The JPT and components must change their paradigm in order to place the full weight of the air component against strategic and long-range strike targets for defined periods and then transition the full weight of the air component against the COG via close air support and interdiction as the land component prepares to make contact. An evolution from the historical parsing of air power must occur where once the JPT identifies the operational COG, the joint components integrate to place full weight of air and land against it. The joint force must then identify when the COG has been affected and be able to shift to the next priority.

The location where the full weight of close air support are used to penetrate the A2/AD environment and mass against the enemies forces will more than likely be an

---

[18] Ibid.

[19] Ibid., III-24.

operational decisive point.[20] Joint Publication 5-0 describes a decisive point as "a geographic place, specific key event, critical factor, or function that, when acted upon, allows a commander to gain a marked advantage over an adversary or contributes materially to achieving success."[21] The JPT in coordination with the components should identify the location and/or timing of such a decisive point and plan shaping operations to facilitate the effects against it.

In terms of close air support, the identification of a decisive point should allow the air component to shift from a long-range campaign to fully supporting operations with the land component. In order to ensure the joint force is prepared to exert its efforts against the decisive points, objectives, and center of gravity, the JPT should factor in the need for the components to anticipate the shift in operations, arrange operations for synchronization, and align the proper forces and functions.[22]

Anticipation is especially critical for the air component. The air component will need to transition from operations against long-range targets to fully integrating in with the land component. It is critical the air component anticipates when these transitions will occur so it quickly re-roles its forces accordingly. The land component will also need to anticipate but from a different vantage point. The land component will need to anticipate when and where it will make contact with the enemy in order to allow the air component to be in a position to support its effort. The operational commanders will

---

[20] Ibid., III-26.

[21] Ibid.

[22] Ibid., III-35.

need a relationship that allows the sharing of priorities and support required in order to integrate and achieve the desired effects.

In order to facilitate the relationship between the operational leaders, the JPT should arrange operations and forces and functions in a manner that integrates the land and air component. With the air component transitioning between long-range strike and close air support and the land component making contact and then timing their maneuver to allow for support in the next contact, the operation requires the appropriate sequencing. By phasing effectively, the joint force can attack both the enemies forces and functions in an integrated fashion. Neither the enemies A2/AD threat system nor the smaller force will allow a reactive transition in forces and functions. The integration between the air component and the land component must be proactive in nature to ensure successful execution of the aforementioned key joint principles.

## Joint Functions

With an understanding of the joint principles required for close air support in an A2/AD threat environment with a reduced force size, and the necessary elements of operational design, there are key aspects of the joint functions required for success. The JPT should now develop a COA that ties command and control, movement and maneuver, fires, intelligence, sustainment and protection together.[23] Of these joint

---

[23] Ibid., IV-21.

functions command and control, movement and maneuver, fires, and intelligence are the most critical to close air support.

Historical examples have shown that command and control (C2) has been a continually evolving function within close air support. The current system of command and control provides excellent synthesis for apportionment push and pull close air support. However, in the future the command and control structure will need to support air strike packages transitioning from interdiction and global strike missions to close air support expeditiously and efficiently. The operational plan in conjunction with the C2 should allow forces the authority to rapidly transition between strike and support. Without that overarching intent, the C2 structure has the potential to stagnate and slow down the air component's transitions or negatively influence the land components ability to synchronize their movements.

The movement and maneuver function holds a significant importance for the land component. Recent conflicts have shown situations where the ground force is unable to wait for the effects of airpower prior to their movement to contact. If the operational environment will not allow the air component to shape the environment in preparation for the land force, the land forces movement and maneuver must be coordinated with the effects of air power. Simply, the land component must surge and pause while integrated with the air component in order to be effective.

The joint force must integrate its fires much more comprehensively in order to be effective, especially from the vantage of air power. Capabilities have a considerable impact on the ability to operate in an A2/AD environment and provide the necessary support to achieve the desired effects. In order for the air component to be effective, the

JPT will not be able to partition off a percentage of assets to provide support for the land component as part of a fires plan. In this proposed future environment, the JPT must plan and anticipate using the entire spectrum of air power against the enemy in not only long-range strike missions but also close air support. In essence, the air component must take traditional long-range strike packages and turn them into A2/AD close air support packages. The full weight of the air component is the only way to support the ground force in order to meet the operational objectives.

Finally, intelligence must evolve its priorities to support an integrated land and air component executing close air support. While the individual components have prioritized intelligence appropriately to support their functions and tasks, an integrated priority of intelligence tasks will enhance close air support and the arrangement of operations leading up to air power supporting the land force.

Detailed planning and integration will be critical to an effective operational plan. The JPT must continually reference the joint principles, elements of operational design, and joint functions in order to be successful. Effective integration and the role of close air support must be a priority or the joint force will increase its risk in reaching a military end state. To ensure integration is paramount, the operational leadership must have the proper relationships in place throughout the planning process and execution.

# CHAPTER 4: PERSONALTIES AND RELATIONSHIPS

While the JPT's operational plan is critical success, the relationship between the operational leaders is the key factor upon which everything hinges. The historical review of the leaders who implemented close air support shows a spectrum of relations ranging from dysfunctional to synergistic. From the poor relationship examples of General Almond's distrust of the air component to beneficial relationships exhibited by General Hostage's most recent "commit everything" to the land component, the relations between leaders will make the difference in the future operational environment.

Historically, at the tactical level, ground forces have always appreciated air support and congruently, fighter-bomber pilots have gone to extraordinary lengths to protect troops on the ground. Operational planners have attempted to design and refine systems in an attempt to create a network that effectively requests, tasks, accurately apportions, and operationally executes JCAS. If tactical motivation between ground and air operators is high and operational systems are always evolving to more effective constructs, then operational leadership will be the defining factor for success in a more lethal environment.

Operational leaders from all services have struggled with a dichotomy of competing demands. Air component leaders have struggled to determine whether their role is to win the war via the air component's strategic strikes or to support the land component's campaign. Conversely, land component leaders debate whether they are able to defeat another ground force autonomously or whether they are dependent upon air power for help. As the joint force moves forward to an environment where air power will

71

not always be available "on demand" and the land component still requires support, sound operational leadership is required to overcome the resulting friction and tensions.

## Intent and Trust

Joint Publication 5-0 defines the Commander's Intent as a statement that contains purpose, end state, and risk.[1] The intent that is critical to the success of close air support in future joint operations is much more personal than just an intent statement. At its most basic level, intent is the true meaning or purpose behind one's actions or statements. It is the ability to convey that your statements or actions are not for one's own benefit, but to serve others.[2] Intent is the first tenet of leadership principles because it will dictate how the most fundamental interactions between the land component and the air component will occur.

Intent may seem like a basic or self-explanatory key factor, but unfortunately, history has shown that operational leader's intent has been either to further their service's doctrine, push their own agenda, or disregard what is best for the overall campaign in favor of their own dogmatic ideology. As the joint planning team initiates planning actions, they will begin to conceptualize the roles and functions of the components with the associated tasks in their respective domains. This initial conceptualization is rooted in the combatant commander's operational art and resultant approach for the operational

---

[1] U.S. Joint Chiefs of Staff, *Joint Operation Planning,* Joint Publication 5-0 (Washington, D.C.: Joint Chiefs of Staff, 11 August 2011), A-5.

[2] Stephen M.R. Covey with Rebecca R. Merrill, *The Speed of Trust* (New York: Free Press, 2006), 78.

plan. Intent carries such significant importance because it is the nested relationship supporting the CCDR's vision.

If the CCDR envisions a campaign, where the primary stakeholder responsible for the main line of effort is the air component, the land component commander must account for this in his ensuing operations, actions, and expected support requirements. Conversely, if the main line of effort is the land component, it must be the air component's intent to prioritize supporting missions over other possible actions. This may seem self-evident, but again as the historical examples cited, there are many cases where an air component or land components actions did not align with their stated intent. It is crucial for the land and air components via their mission statement, commander's intent, and supporting tasks, to communicate and execute integrated support to the other component in order to be successful.

Within a higher threat environment, with a smaller multi-role air corps, if actions do not align with intent, the results could be catastrophic. In a low threat environment, with mass and specialized mission support, there is the availability to have periods of misalignment of intent and actions, while still being able to recover operationally. The same is not true for the A2/AD future operational environment. If the land component pushes into an engagement area during a period when the conditions are optimal for the air component to execute strikes or the land component executes its movement to contact and the air component has not transitioned from long-range strike to close air support, culmination or failure could be the result. Each operational service leader needs to be true in stating his or her intent to support the other. Intent is a foundational concept the strategic leader must embrace in order to be successful and that will in turn facilitate trust between the two components.

Within this new model of operational planning and priorities, one can foresee that trust may initially be a "soft" key factor. In the most recent conflicts, the components built trust not only through their actions but also through their presence. Low threat environments allowed air support to loiter over engagement areas or arrive rapidly on-station should the need arrive. Sporadic engagements also meant that if there were any need for close air support, determining the prioritization was relatively simply because there were no other competing priorities in the battle-space.

In this possible new environment, persistent presence is not a viable option. The threat and numerous competing priorities mean that there will be durations of time air support is not readily available. The land component must understand at the tactical level, due to a higher threat environment the time to attack, and time between attacks, will be much greater in length than in recent history. These factors may be initially unsettling to a land component in hostile territory.

That is why trust between operational component leaders is essential. If there are fractures in the trust between the components at any stage of execution, it will have a detrimental effect on an exponential scale. The land component must have the assurance that when the priority shifts to support for the air component, the forces will be available to execute. The air component must also trust that the land component will make their air support requests at times when the effects from air power will have the greatest impact on the engagement area.

Trust will be essential to reaching the campaign plans military end-states, but in building that trust and working towards the end-states, each component will need to prioritize their roles and missions accurately. The operational leaders may have unwavering trust in one another, but if they are unable to prioritize their effects in a manner that influences the center of gravity, their trust and intent will not yield a victory.

## Prioritization

The operational commanders must prioritize their effects, objectives, and decisive points in order to be successful. Historical examples have shown cases where the integration between the air component and land component has devolved due to the inability to update their priorities. The priorities of air support and land component timing and synchronization will change from day to day, possibly even several times a day. Prioritization will begin in the operational planning between the two component commanders.

Operational leaders must agree upon a construct for the arranging operations, sequencing, and synchronization for both components' execution.[3] Then, planners must construct a framework of air component priorities simultaneously with the land components priorities. This framework will carry the forces forward into execution. It is essential leaders communicate which component has the priority throughout the campaign so there is a shared understanding amongst all the forces. The pre-planned

---

[3] U.S. Joint Chiefs of Staff, *Joint Operation Planning*, III-35.

priorities will allow the operational and tactical actions to execute with mission command for a majority of the operations.

However, there will be times when an emerging situation, meeting engagement, troops-in-contact, that will necessitate a rapid shift in priorities. The adversary actions, environmental conditions, technological issues, and other unforeseen events will require rapid and decisive re-prioritization. The possibility of rapid re-prioritization reinforces the need for developing a pre-existing framework in planning that facilitates air and land integration. Re-prioritization for multiple agencies is far more effective when deviating from a known plan or point vice attempting to generate a new plan. Essential to success is the requirement to have already built into the plan, the communication, receipt, acknowledgement, and execution when re-prioritization occurs. These procedures should be understood and executable from the tactical level up to the strategic level and from the strategic level down to the tactical level.

An example of transitioning priorities in a future conflict may entail an air component's shift from long-range strike package to emerging close air support requirements. As the air component executes its tasks and achieves its effects it will need to have awareness of the land components intent and priorities. When the land component is executing a movement or maneuver, the air component should wield its mass and effects against long-range strike targets. As the land component nears a meeting engagement, decisive point, or objective the air component needs to shift its priority to support the ground force. This shift needs to happen proactively in preparation for land force engagement and reactively if a chance meeting engagement should occur.

With the smaller air component and robust threat, there is an increased potential that the JFACC and JFLCC will need to shift their priorities several times throughout a campaign. Prioritization will be increasingly more dynamic for future operations, but it is necessary to maximize mission effectiveness for the land and air Component.

## Possible Doctrinal Mission Degradation

Each component will have a desire to execute their core functions at the highest level of execution as possible. Unfortunately, with a smaller force in a higher threat, there will be periods where shifting priorities will cause that effectiveness to degrade. Doctrinally when engaging an adversary, the air component has prioritized strategic strikes to create effects that will allow ground forces to reach its objectives against an enemy force that is without sustainment, infrastructure, or command and control.[4]

The apportionment model solved the struggle between strategic effect and support in the past. In the apportionment model, a percentage of the Air Tasking Order executes JCAS, which allows strategic strikes to go on without interruption. This model allows both core functions to occur without a degradation of doctrinal mission sets. The components must enter into future operations with the shared understanding that the operational environment of more lethal threats and a smaller more multi-role air component will degrade their historical doctrinal effectiveness, and therefore they are accepting greater risk.

---

[4] U.S. Air Force, *Air Force Doctrine Document 1: Air Force Basic Doctrine, Organization, and Command* (Washington, D.C.: U.S. Air Force, 14 October 2011), 19.

Leaders must understand this assumption, convey that understanding to the JPT, and accept the level of component mission degradation in order to reach a higher level of operational effectiveness. While this loss of effectiveness might be disconcerting to leaders and planners, using Joint concepts and principles, forces can mitigate and minimize the degradation.

In a future campaign, the land component may desire an approach that focuses on rapid movement to contact at an objective or decisive point. Due to the constraints of force size and the support the air component can provide, the land component may need to compromise and execute an operational pause to allow air power to shift from strike missions to close air support. Conversely, the approach for the air component may include overwhelming and persistent attacks on command and control, leadership, and infrastructure. The JFACC may need to temper that approach with a pause in strikes to mass a close air support "strike package" and support the ground force.

The historical examples have shown some of the greatest frictions degrading Joint effectiveness have come during a dogmatic adherence to service doctrine versus a Joint approach. A successful plan incorporating the Joint principles, elements of operational design, and joint functions is the first step in integrating to achieve a synergistic effect. The foundation to that integration is operational leaders who understand the need for joint execution. It is essential the JFC, JFACC, and JFLCC lead the effort by ensuring the relationship between the air component and land component facilitate close air support.

# CONCLUSION

History is replete with divisions between the land and air component that have led to the ineffectiveness of close air support. As the operational environment evolves, it is critical the joint force apply the successful tenets of operational planning and leadership in order to be effective. Smaller force size, anti-access/area denial, and existing paradigms of persistent and unabated close air support could all culminate in an inability to meet operational objectives. The air component finds itself completing a full revolution in aircraft design versus roles and functions as the economic environment has dictated the force must be multi-role. The land component has stripped its capability of organic fire support in favor of a smaller and more mobile force structure. It is imperative the joint force evolve with the changing operational environment to ensure success. Planning and executing close air support cannot be a simplistic methodology of apportionment or improvised re-tasking. There cannot be a division between operational leaders and their expectations for air and land integration. If operational leaders are not in alignment with their priorities and the joint planning team does not account for the increased threat with a smaller force, results far more deadly and disastrous than Operation ANACONDA will occur. Operation ANACONDA exemplifies the misalignment between operational planning and the failure of operational leadership, which in an A2/AD environment will have deadly consequences. In order to meet the demands of this future environment the joint force must be diligent in its relationships between operational leaders and the joint planning teams approach to planning.

Joint leaders and operational planning teams need to incorporate the successful

tenets from Bradley and Quesada, Montgomery and Coningham, Patton and Weyland,

Schwarzkopf and Horner, and Petraeus and Hostage to ensure joint integration is

successful.  In order to accomplish these ends, the joint planning team must proactively

identify the need for close air support when assessing the operational environment and

determining an operational approach.  The team must facilitate the JFC's guidance and

intent by ensuring integration between the air and land component is present at the

inception of operational planning.  A proactive joint planning team anticipating the need

for robust close air support planning will not only set the conditions to strengthen the

relationship between the land and air component commander, but should also ensure

operational close air support planning is detailed throughout plan development.

Currently, within *Chairman of the Joint Chiefs of Staff Manual 3130.03, Adaptive*

*Planning and Execution Planning Formats and Guidance* dated 18 October 2012, which

directs the guidance, format, and contents for operational plans, of the 593 pages of

instruction there is not a reference for the joint integration of close air support between

the land and air component.[1]  While, the joint manual does cover a myriad of topics

ranging from dynamic targeting to combat camera, due to the joint nature of close air

support and the detailed level of planning required in order to ensure successfulness, it is

highly recommended to incorporate a new joint close air support Tab.  The joint nature

and collaboration between the air and ground components suggests that merely

---

[1] U.S. Joint Chiefs of Staff, *Adaptive Planning and Execution (APEX) Planning Formats and Guidance*, Chairman of the Joint Chiefs of Staff Manual 3130.03 (Washington, D.C.: Joint Chiefs of Staff, 18 October 2012), 1 - 2.

incorporating close air support into a component's section is insufficient. By creating a close air support section within the operational plan, the joint planning team should put forth the required level of planning in order to reach the necessary level of integration. A proposed location for this new tab would reside in Annex C Operations, Appendix 6 Joint Fire Support, in a newly created Tab G titled <u>Joint Close Air Support</u>.[2]

With the addition of a dedicated home for joint close air support within an operational plan, the planning team will be able to better communicate the key factors critical to successful JCAS operational planning in a future environment. The joint planning team can then ensure the joint principles of mass, maneuver, offensive, and simplicity are incorporated into the approach. During operational design, the team can determine the ways close air support is wielded against enemy centers of gravity, decisive points, while anticipating operational sequencing and phasing. As the plan gains greater fidelity the team can then use the joint functions of command and control, movement and maneuver, fires, and intelligence to ensure close air support is successful. With the operational planning acting as the foundation, operational leadership is the overarching direction guiding close air support.

Operational leaders need to foster and display a relationship that is founded in trust to influence the rest of the joint force. Leadership will shape an environment that facilitates an understanding of how and when the components will transition their priorities. The operational leaders must work together in an integrated relationship that has a shared understanding of when the land component is the supported priority to when

---

[2] U.S. Joint Chiefs of Staff, *Adaptive Planning and Execution*, E-C-111.

a transition occurs and the land component must pause so the air component can take on the role of main effort. Only then, can the joint force balance its capability to interdict long-range strategic strike with supporting a maneuvering ground force.

To ensure operational leaders are prepared for these operational transitions, the joint force should transition away from component exercises like *Red Flag* and the *National Training Center* to large-scale joint exercises. These exercises should include the joint force standing up a joint planning team, the creation of an operational plan, and within execution, the shifts from land component priorities to air component priorities. Only through habitual training at the operational level, will critical relationships between services form and synthesize.

The future of close air support is dependent upon a dedicated, thinking, and integrated joint force. It is critical that the key tenets presented within this paper are not learned or realized during execution, but are anticipated and implemented early in the planning process. The success of the next joint campaign requires joint planners who are historically minded and are able to implement joint principles and functions. In turn, those joint planners need to have operational leadership that understands the critical importance of the relationships that make successful close air support possible.

# BIBLIOGRAPHY

## Books

Anderegg, C.R. *Sierra Hotel:  Flying Air Force Fighters in the Decade After Vietnam.* Washington, D.C.: Air Force History and Museums Program, 2001.

Call, Steve. *Danger Close:  Tactical Air Controllers in Afghanistan and Iraq.* College Station, TX: Texas A&M University Press, 2007.

Clancy, Tom and Chuck Horner. *Every Man a Tiger: The Gulf War Campaign.* New York: Berkley Books, 2005.

Cooling, B. Franklin and United States Air Force, Office of Air Force History. *Case Studies in the Development of Close Air Support.* Washington, D.C.: Office of Air Force History, U.S. Air Force, 1990.

Covey, Stephen M. R., and Rebecca R. Merrill. *The Speed of Trust : The One Thing That Changes Everything.* New York: Free Press, 2008.

Douhet, Giulio. *The Command of the Air.* Washington, D.C.: Office of Air Force History, 1983.

Franks, Tommy, and Malcolm McConnell. *American Soldier.* New York: Regan Books, 2004.

Grau, Lester W. and Dodge Billingsley. *Operation ANACONDA: America's First Major Battle in Afghanistan.* Lawrence, KA: University Press of Kansas, 2011.

Hughes, Thomas A. *Overlord: General Pete Quesada and the Triumph of Tactical Air Power in World War II.* New York:  Free Press, 1995.

Jamieson, Perry D. *Lucrative targets: The U.S. Air Force in the Kuwaiti Theater of Operations.* Washington, D.C.: Air Force History and Museums Program, 2001.

Leonhard, Robert R. *The Art of Maneuver: Maneuver-Warfare Theory and AirLand Battle.* Novato, CA: Presidio Press, 1991.

Locher, James R. *Victory on the Potomac:  The Goldwater-Nichols Act Unifies the Pentagon.* College Station: Texas A&M University Press, 2002.

MacPherson, Malcolm. *Roberts Ridge:  A Story of Courage and Sacrifice on Takur Ghar Mountain, Afghanistan.* New York: Delacorte Press, 2005.

McGrath, John J. *Fire for Effect: Field Artillery and Close Air Support in the US Army*. Fort Leavenworth, KS: Combat Studies Institute Press, 2010.

Murray, Williamson, and Robert H. Scales. *The Iraq War: A Military History*. Cambridge, MA: Belknap Press of Harvard University Press, 2003.

Perrett, Geoffery. *There is a War to be Won*. New York: Random House, 1991.

Naylor, Sean. *Not a Good Day to Die : The Untold Story of Operation ANACONDA*. New York: Berkley Books, 2005.

Reynolds, Richard T. *Heart of the Storm : The Genesis of the Air Campaign Against Iraq*. Maxwell Air Force Base, AL: Air University Press, 1995.

Schlight, John. *Help from Above : Air Force Close Air Support of the Army 1946-1973*. Washington, D.C.: Air Force History and Museums Program, 2003.

Schwarzkopf, H. Norman, and Peter Petre. *It Doesn't Take a Hero*. New York: Bantam Books, 1992.

Warden, John A. *The Air Campaign : Planning for Combat*. Washington, D.C.: National Defense University Press, 1990.

Theses, Dissertations, and Papers

Lewis, Michael. Lt Gen Ned Almond, USA A Ground Commander's Conflicting View with Airmen Over CAS Doctrine and Employment. Master's thesis, Air University, 1997.

U.S. Government Documents and Websites

Department of Defense. *Sustaining U.S. Global Leadership: Priorities for 21$^{st}$ Century Defense* Washington, D.C.: U.S. Department of Defense, January 2012.

U.S. Air Force. *Air Force Doctrine Document 1 Air Force Basic Doctrine, Organization, and Command*. Washington, D.C.: U.S. Air Force, 14 October 2011.

U.S. Air Force. "An Executive Brief on the Development of Close Air Support Doctrine." Headquarters Tactical Air Command: Doctrine Division Directorate of Concepts Doctrine Policy and Studies, 5 January 1972.

U.S. Air Force. *Counterland Operations*, Air Force Doctrine Document 3-03, Washington, D.C.: U.S. Air Force, 11 September 2006, Change 1 28 July 2008.

U.S. Air Force. "Operation ANACONDA An Air Power Perspective." Washington, D.C.: Headquarters, Air Force AF/XOL, 7 February 2005.

U.S. Army. "A Short History of Close Air Support Issues." Fort Belvoir, VA: Headquarters, U.S. Army Combat Development Command Institute of Special Studies, 1 July 1968.

U.S. Joint Chiefs of Staff. *Adaptive Planning and Execution (APEX) Planning Formats and Guidance,* Chairman of the Joint Chiefs of Staff Manual 3130.03. Washington, D.C.: Joint Chiefs of Staff, 18 October 2012.

U.S. Joint Chiefs of Staff. *Joint Operations*, Joint Publication 3-0. Washington, D.C.: Joint Chiefs of Staff, 11 August 2011.

U.S. Joint Chiefs of Staff. *Joint Airspace Control*, Joint Publication 3-52. Washington, D.C.: Joint Chiefs of Staff, 20 March 2010.

U.S. Joint Chiefs of Staff. *Joint Operation Planning*, Joint Publication 5-0. Washington, D.C.: Joint Chiefs of Staff, 11 August 2011.


Newspaper, Magazine, and Wire Service Articles, including online

Grant, Rebecca. "Airpower in a Fragmented Battlespace." *Air Force Magazine*, July 2006, http://www.airforcemag.com/MagazineArchive/Pages/2006/July%202006/0706ba ttlespace.aspx (Accessed 24 April 2013).

_____. "Marine Air in the Mainstream." *Air Force Magazine*, June 2004, http://www.airforcemag.com/MagazineArchive/Pages/2004/June%202004/0604m arine.aspx (Accessed 24 April 2013).

Freier,Nathan. "The Emerging Anti-Access/Area Denial Challenge."*Center of Strategic and International Studies*, 17 May 2012, http://csis.org/publication/emerging-anti-accessarea-denial-challenge (Accessed 18 January 2013).

Schanz, Mark V. "Committing everything to the battlefield." *Air Force Magazine*, July 2011, http://www.airforcemag.com/MagazineArchive/Pages/2011/July%202011/0711ba ttlefield.aspx (Accessed 24 April 2013).

Schogol, Jeff. "5 A-10 squadrons to be cut, Tight budgets lead AF to focus on F-35 capabilities." *Air Force Times*, 30 January 2012, http://www.airforcetimes.com/article/20120130/NEWS/201300303/5-A-10-squadrons-to-be-cut (Accessed 17 January 2013)